PUTTING IT ALL TOGETHER

World Conquest, Global Genocide and African Liberation

Terrance Jackson

Published by

U.B. & U.S. COMMUNICATIONS SYSTEMS, INC
912 West Pembroke Ave ● Hampton, Va 23669
(804)723-2696

SECOND EDITION ● SECOND PRINTING
AUGUST 1994

ISBN # 1-56411-090 -7   YBBG # 0098

Printed in the United States of America
By
U. B. & U. S. Communications Systems, Inc.
912 West Pembroke Ave.
Hampton, Virginia 23669
(804)723-2696

To

The youths who go hungry and are sacrificed in the name of profit and productivity. While you suffer the emporer grows fat from avarice. May you acquire the courage and the wisdom to proclaim that the emporer is naked.

Escape from the Labyrinth
Terrance Jackson

To the creatures born of cruelty and greed
And trapped in the dreaded labyrinth by the tyrant
Freedom from the labyrinth cannot be granted
It can only be taken

Those who are strong and courageous enough
To live in the terrifying world of reality
And not rely on the comforts of illusions
Remembering that the spiritual world is as real
As the world of matter and mass
Need only close their eyes
And the labyrinth shall be gone

A force permeates in every living being
And only those who respect this force
Shall rule their kingdoms
For the power within is the greatest power of all
Once obtained and tamed
It shall be omnipotent
And enable you to do what you will
Yet it shall be impotent
And leave you unable to determine what you will

Men and women are continually tempted
With the seeds of their own destruction
And the continuous cycle
Of birth, life and death goes on

TABLE OF CONTENTS

ACKNOWLEDGEMENTS

I would like to thank my mother, Lezile Linder and my step-father, Floyd Linder who have made this book possible. I would also like to thank all the writers and researchers, too numerous to name, who I used as a foundation to build this piece of work upon. I would also like to especially thank the "Numbers and You" man, Lloyd Strayhorn, for giving me the opportunity to be on his show.

Please note that the facts and conclusions contain in this book are meant to be challenge. Only when we are challenged do we learn. And remember, as you read through this book that thinking is allowed and encouraged.

CHAPTER 1

OUT OF THE WILDERNESS

> I came into a place void of all light,
> which bellows like the sea in tempest,
> when it is combated by warring winds....
> This miserable state is borne by the
> wretched souls of those who lived
> without disgrace and without praise.
>
> Dante Alighieri

Are the "powers that be" deliberately trying to destroy Black people? If someone would have asked me that question in 1990, I would have answered: Of course not, you're just being paranoid. But now, my thoughts on the matter have greatly shifted. Of course, I realized back in 1990 that Black people were being destroyed, but for me to say that it was deliberate and not because of apathy was going a bit too far. In this age of "enlightenment" and "racial equality," I felt no one with the power to do so, would be that devious or that sinister. I felt that the destruction of Black people may be the dream of a few right-wing radicals or neo-Nazis but I felt the majority of the people in power were sane, rational human beings. They might not be too concern for Black people but I would have found it very hard to believe that they were deliberately trying to kill us off. But faced with the overwhelming evidence it has become painfully apparent that the "powers that be" are engaged in

1

nothing less than massive genocide on a global scale in their attempt to control the world.

The Peace Corps and Southern Africa

My story on how my views on the deliberate massive global genocide that is being perpetrated by the "powers that be" starts in the latter part of 1990. I was scheduled to go to southern Africa to teach math in the Peace Corps. In an attempt to better prepare myself for this experience I started to do some research on the region and on U.S. foreign policy. From this research, I stumbled across some shocking facts about U.S. foreign policy in regards to southern Africa. During my research, it became clear to me that the foreign policy's goal for the region is to keep the region destabilized using many of the methods, such as, "low-intensity" warfare, political assassinations, and currency destabilization, that were used to destabilized the nations of Southeast Asia, i.e., Vietnam, Laos, and Cambodia.

As if that revelation wasn't shocking enough, I also learned that the Central Intelligence Agency (CIA) plotted to assassinate Patrice Lumumba, founder of the National Congolese Movement. This man was a hero to me and millions of others all over the world, and was destined to be one the greatest leaders of post-colonial Africa. The fact that the CIA planned an assassination is supported by the findings of a U.S. Senate select committee report given in November 1975. This committee also revealed that the CIA plotted to assassinate Fidel Castro of Cuba, and that American officials had been directly involved with the killers of Vietnamese President Ngo Dinh Diem, Chilean General Rene Schneider and dictator Rafael Trujilo of the Dominican Republic.

From this new knowledge that I had acquire, I was starting to wake-up and realize the true nature of those monsters called Western Imperialism and White Supremacy. And about two weeks before I was to leave for Africa some unexpected dental problems popped up and I was unable to go to Africa with my original group. This delay gave me a little time to think and after a little soul searching, I decided against going into the Peace Corps. I figured if I am ever fortunate enough to go home to Africa, I will do so on my own terms and not on the terms of a government whose goals in the region are suspect. Since I was no longer going to Africa at this time, I was left unemployed and uncertain of what direction my life would take next. I was definitely lost in the wilderness.

Life Under the Tree (A Metaphoric Tale)

During this trip into the wilderness I began to recall past experiences in the dark forest. On my previous trip I journeyed for a long time in the wilderness and that is when I came upon this tree. It was a big, beautiful tree and it had three letters etched into its bark - *I*, *B*, and *M*. The spirits that lived in the tree told me that I was welcomed to rest here under the tree and it would shelter me and the fruit from the tree would nourish me. I was weary and the offer was very tempting, so I decided that I would rest under the tree, at least for awhile until I got my strength back. I ate the fruit from the tree and it was indeed very tasty but I didn't realize that it was also drugged; it made me forget the voices of my ancestors. My Odyssey became that of Ulysses in the land of the lotus-eaters. But life was happy under the tree, well at least I thought it was. In the beginning the fruit from this tree seemed to satisfy my every hunger, yet something - something I could not quite explain - was left unfed.

One day while I was enjoying the shelter of the tree there came a terrible storm. Thunder and lightning so powerful that it seem to shake the whole earth. Then out in the distance, images began to form. "Askia! Sundiata! Shyaam! Shaka! Is that you?" "*Impi ebomvu*!" was the reply.[1]   As   the storm continued to rage all around me I suddenly realized how unhappy life had actually been under this tree. Then the storm began to subside but in its wake it had forged a path where no path existed before. Where this path ends is uncertain but what is certain is the unhappiness at the beginning of the path. So here I stand at the beginning of a path whose end is unknown; but before I attempt the journey, I must first chop a few trees down or at least trim some branches to make kindling for a fire that will help guide the journey.

Why I Wrote This Book

I am not writer by profession or by training but only a man who believes that he has something of importance to say to his people and sees writing as an effective tool to get a message out. I just see too many people walking around who just don't understand what is going on. This makes me frighten about the ultimate destiny of African people, those at home and those abroad. My fear is most aptly reflected in the words of one of the great leaders of African Nationalism in the 1950s and 60s, Carlos Cooks:

> The largest true minority in the United States of America, "the black people," or people of African blood and descent, ARE - and will continue to be the Vagabonds and Clowns of American Society. Their position in the scheme of things, and their inability to understand the evil designs of White Psychology, has reduced the black people into an economic liability, a

[1] "Strike an enemy once and for all. Let him cease to exist as a tribe or he will live to fly at your throat again." If, he [Shaka] said, there must be war, let it be *impi ebomvu* - total war. But treat generously those who submit without war. Ritter, E.A. Shaka Zulu (Penguin Books, London, 1955).

social loser, and a political nonentity. And as long as they continue to pursue the foolish phantom of amalgamation and integration as the absolute solution to all their problems, they shall continue to be the group that furnishes victims for the lynch mobs, targets for the policeman's bullet, customers for the narcotic peddlers, concubines for degenerate whitemen, and general footstools for the rest of the American public to inflate their ego on.

This book is an attempt to give Black people a better understanding of the world around them. My hope is that this will help people of African descent realize that it is fruitless to continue to beat down those same old tired paths of integration and legal remedies in our pursuit of liberty. I also hope to give to my African brothers and sisters of the Diaspora a better understanding of the extremely complicated world in which we live before we attempt to journey down paths unknown. It is a tragic but accurate fact that the vast majority of Black people do not have the first clue as to why things happen the way that they happen. They take at full face-value the things they are told by politicians and our so-called leaders. And as Brother Malcolm would put it, they're going east when they think they're going west and going west when they think they're going east.

I must admit that until recently I was a bit off course myself. Until recently I was not fully aware of the truly sinister things that the U.S. government and the "powers that be" that control the U.S. government and most of the rest of the world are capable of doing. My research which originally started on southern Africa and then expanded in many other directions brought me to a higher level of awareness of the true nature of the world in which we live. And I would like to share that improved awareness with all my brothers and sisters but especially with those "Negroes" who live deep in the dark forest and never hear those ancestral voices.

The Nigger Problem

So what do I mean when I say that the "powers that be" are deliberately trying to destroy Black people? What I mean is that "powers that be" along with their efforts to control the world, they also feel that their white world would be a much better place without Black people. Let's examine some facts:

o The life expectancy for Blacks is decreasing while it is increasing for whites.
o The Black infant mortality rate is rapidly increasing, the infant mortality rate in some Black communities in the U.S. is higher than that of many so-called Third World countries.
o Blacks only represent about 13% of the U.S. population, yet they represent over 50% of new AIDS victims.
o Police officers are shooting and killing Black people at an alarming rate.
o Black people are shooting and killing Black people at an alarming rate.
o 1 out of 4 Black males between the ages of 20 and 29 are caught in the web of the criminal justice system.
o Black males are imprisoned at a rate four times that of Black males in South Africa: 3,109 out of every 100,000, as compared to 729.
o There are more Black males of college age in prison than there are in colleges and universities.

There can be no denying that Black people are being destroyed, but the important questions are: Why? And by whom?

The main reason for this destruction is that Black people have become obsolete to the Western world. Western-industrialized nations are now moving towards the 21st century and Black labor as well as other non-white labor is steadily being replaced with machines and 21st-century technology. Modern production is no longer dependent on the cheap labor of the "masses." And to white people Black people have never been seen as human beings but only as a problem: The "nigger" problem and "the only good nigger is a dead nigger." This attitude is very apparent in Sidney M. Wilhelm's *Who Needs the Negro*:

> White America may readily admit to its racism without any qualms; it suffers from no misgivings when adhering even to the most extreme advocacy, namely, genocide. In disposing of an unwanted race, whites avoid pangs of compunction simply by confessing to the submission of racism in accord with the absolutes in the myths of racism...America is a white nation marking time for black people. After centuries of advance, the white majority repudiates the black minority for the very conditions it is itself to blame: poverty, ignorance, family disruption, filth, crime, disease, substandard housing, incompetence, lack of initiative. While assuring majestic prospects for acceptance the nation removes the basic opportunities for achievement; now that the Negro bursts forth with insurrections whites reciprocate with more massive violence until resisting Negroes are fully suppressed. The white strategy reflects an earlier period when "the ingenious plan evolved of first maddening the Indians into war and then falling upon them with exterminating punishment", all along branding the latter with the charge of aggression.

The Whites are the Bitter Enemy

As we move towards the 21st century, we must realize that white people have no intention of peacefully coexisting with Black people. All talk of peaceful coexistence is just a deception to pacify Black people and make our destruction that much easier. If we study our history, we will realize that these current techniques of pacification are the same techniques that Europeans and Arabs have been using on Africans for thousands of years. If we study our history then the only possible conclusion that we can reach is the same conclusion Chancellor Williams reached in his *The Destruction of Black Civilization: Great Issues of a Race from 4500 B.C. to 2000 A.D.*:

> One of the most troublesome fact in the study of history over long periods of times, such as several centuries, is that a truth may slowly emerge, period after period, until it clearly forms itself into a truth impregnable, a fact nowhere explicitly stated as such in the mass of data covered. As one continues to move down through the centuries, countless events and situations may continue to make supporting additions to what has already been established as an unassailable fact. Yet the that truth may be so repugnant, so utterly void of any rational or intelligent reason for its existence, that hardly any historian would wish to state it in his work.
> Yet I did just that when I wrote that "the whites are the implacable foe, the traditional and everlasting enemy of the Blacks." The compelling reason for publicly putting this declaration in its historical context is clear: The necessary re-education of Blacks and a possible solution of racial crises can begin, strangely enough, only when Blacks fully realize this central fact in their lives: *The white man is their Bitter Enemy.* For this is not the ranting of wild-eyed militancy, but the calm and unmistakable verdict of several thousands years of documented history. Even the sample case-study of ten black states [Ethiopia, Makuria, Alwa, Ghana, Mali, Songhay, the Mossi States, Kongo, Angola, and Kuba] in this work shows that each and every one of those states was destroyed by whites. [Emphasis original.]

Once we all come to this realization then we will stop trying to follow the path of acceptance and integration and begin to follow the path of redemption and self-development. LET'S WAKE UP FOLKS AND SMELL THE GRITS!!!

The Hegelian Dialectic

Besides the fact that Blacks are not wanted or needed the destruction of Black people also serves a secondary, more subtle function, that function being to manipulate and impose social change on the general public through hatreds, prejudices, and fears. Georg Wilhelm Friedrich Hegel, a German philosopher, conceived a theory on how to create change in a society. This theory is known as the Hegelian Dialectic where change occurs in a three-step process: thesis, antithesis, and synthesis. The first step (thesis) is to create a problem (AIDS, war, drugs, crime, etc.). The second step (antithesis) is to generate opposition to that problem (fear, panic, hatred, prejudice). The third step (synthesis) is to offer the solution to the problem generated in step one; a change that would not have been possible without the proper psychological conditioning of the first two steps.

Using the principles of the Hegelian Dialectic the "powers that be" are able to use the problems that exist in Black communities to create so much fear that it is easily able to impose its will on the general public. Take for example crime, the media hype on crime is so great and causes so much fear that people become convinced that they must give up certain rights or liberties to combat this problem. Violations of rights such as police harassment, curfews, and illegal searches become tolerable (especially when imposed on Black people) because the general opinion is that the problems are so great that these violations are necessary to combat the problem.

Most of this fear, hatred, and prejudice is directed towards Blacks. Blacks are constantly being portrayed in the media as deviant low-lives not fit to walk on this planet. Just the mere mention of a Black person can send shivers up a white spine. Does anyone remember Willie Horton? Whites declare open season and it becomes okay to kill to a Black person because "these people are just not human." Yusef Hawkins! Does this ring a bell for anyone?

The Power Elites and World Conquest

Who are these "powers that be" that are engaged in massive global genocide? Are they just some abstraction? No, these are real people that walk the face of the earth just like you and me. Most of the people who comprise the "powers that be" can be identified with a little research, if you know what you are looking for. The "powers that be" consist of individuals such as executives of international banking houses, executives of multi-national corporations, partners of prestigious law firms, and high-level government officials. For convenience, I will call this group the international power elites or simply the power elites.

This group of power elites control several prestigious and internationally recognized organizations such as the Council on Foreign Relations, the Trilateral Commission, the Committee for Economic Development, the Business Roundtable, the Ford Foundation, and the Rockefeller Foundation. But the vast majority of their power comes from their control of banking institutions, especially the central banks of various nations. The power elites use their control of banking institutions and various organizations to control governments, public opinion, and economic conditions. This group of power elites is determined to take complete monetary and ultimately, political control of all nations of the earth - quietly, secretly, and, in many cases, in direct violation of the most sacred and lawful agreements (e.g., the U.S. Constitution) set up by these autonomous nations.

Their control and censorship of the communications media has been so firmly established that books and articles revealing the truth about the true aims and objectives of these power elites are never mentioned in such publications as *The New York Times Book Review*. The power elites' control and censorship of the media becomes apparent when one realizes that the media is almost wholly controlled by giant corporations like Time-Warner, CBS, GE (NBC), Capital Cities/ABC - which are in turn controlled largely by banks such as Chase Manhattan and Citibank. The power elites' control of media is supported by Peter Borsan's article "Who Owns the Networks?" (*The Nation*, 25 November 1978). In this article Borsan points out that "Chase and other Rockefeller institutions are among the largest holders of network stock with substantial interests in all three networks [ABC, CBS, NBC]." For example, a 1973 Senate report on disclosure of corporate ownership (issued by Senators Muskie and Metcalf) found that Chase Manhattan controlled 14 percent of CBS. Borsan points out that, with stock widely distributed among shareholders, institutions can wield great influence or outright control with 5 percent, or sometimes 1 or 2 percent, equity.

Despite the power elites' control and censorship of the media there is information available about what is going on "behind the scenes," but it is just a little harder to find. Carroll Quigley, a former professor of history at the Foreign Service School of Georgetown University, shed a great deal of light on what the power elites are really up in 1966 with his *Tragedy and Hope: A History of the World in Our Time*, in which he states:

> I know of the operations of this network [the Council on Foreign Relations] because I have studied it for twenty years and was permitted for two years, in the early 1960's, to examine its papers and secret records. I have no

aversion to it or to most of its aims and have, for much of my life, been close to it and to many of its instruments.... In general, my chief difference of opinion is that it wishes to remain unknown.

And what are these "aims"?

Nothing less than to create a world system of financial control in private hands able to dominate the political system of each country and the economy of the world. This system was to be controlled in a feudalist fashion by the central banks of the world acting in concert by secret meetings and conferences. The apex of the system was to be...a private bank owned and controlled by the world's central banks which themselves are private corporations. Each central bank...sought to dominate its government by its ability to control treasury loans, to manipulate foreign exchanges, to influence the level of economic activity in the country, and to influence cooperative politicians by subsequent economic rewards in the business world.

Carroll Quigley also taught at Harvard and Princeton, and in 1949 he wrote a book called *The Anglo-American Establishment*, which describes the secret society created by Cecil Rhodes. He describes how this secret society was the invisible hand that actually controlled the governments and industries of both the United States and Great Britain. He also revealed that both the Royal Institute of International Affairs in Great Britain and the Council for Foreign Relations in the United States were fronts for this secret society. Even though this book was originally written in 1949, Professor Quigley could not find a publisher until 1981. Even in the preface Professor Quigley tells us that "I have been told that the story I relate here would be better left untold...." Quigley mysteriously died soon after the publication of this book. The following is from the first paragraph of the preface:

The Rhodes Scholarships, established by the terms of Cecil Rhodes's seventh will, are known to everyone. What is not so widely known is that Rhodes in five previous wills left his fortune to form a secret society, which was to devote itself to the preservation and expansion of the British Empire. And what does not seem to be known to anyone is that this secret society was created by Rhodes and his principle trustee, Lord Milner, and continues to exist to this day. To be sure, this secret society is not a childish thing like the Ku Klux Klan, and it does not have any secret robes, secret handclasps, or secret passwords. It does not need any of these, since its members know each other intimately. It probably has no oaths of secrecy nor any formal procedures of initiation. It does, however, exist and holds secret meetings, over which the senior member present presides. At various times since 1891, these meetings have been presided over by Rhodes, Lord Milner, Lord Selborne, Sir Patrick Duncan, Field Marshal Jan Smuts, Lord Lothian, and Lord Brand.

Additional evidence exist of a conspiracy for world control in a document referred to as *The Protocols of the Meetings of the Learned Elders of Zion*. This set of 24 *Protocols* spells out a sinister yet extremely cunning program for world domination. Its program of world domination consist of controlling governments and the public at large by controlling financial institutions and the banking establishment. A copy of these *Protocols* have been in the British Museum since August 10, 1906. What is truly amazing about this document is that it predicted World War I, the Russian Revolution, and the formation of the League of Nations (forerunner to the United Nations). So the person or persons responsible for creating these *Protocols* must have known what they were talking about in order to predict events that would take place decades in the future. [see Appendix A for a copy of Protocol No. 1.]

A Brief History Lesson on Bankers

If you find it hard to believe that bankers can control governments then it would behoove you to take note of the words of Napoleon:

> When a government is dependent for money upon bankers, they and not the leaders of the government control the situation, since the hand that gives is above the hands that takes... Money has no motherland; financiers are without patriotism and without decency; their sole object is gain.

In analyzing this statement you should keep in mind that Napoleon was the crowned Emperor of France and created an empire that covered most of western and central Europe. He was the greatest European military genius of his time. His-story will tell you that Napoleon was in fact the greatest military genius of his time. But those of us who are conscious know who was in fact the greatest military genius of that time. Hint: *impi ebomvu!*

For nearly 20 years, Napoleon's armies crushed foe after foe until he seemed invincible. And yet he claimed that he was helpless against mere bankers. Let's look at some of the facts and determine if Napoleon's fear was warranted. His-story tells us that the Duke of Wellington defeated Napoleon at Waterloo but in reality it was more like a triumph for the international bankers.

In 1815, the British Duke of Wellington was raising an army in the Pyenees mountains (between Spain and France) to lead against Napoleon, and he needed a tremendous amount of gold (some 800,000 British pounds worth) to accomplish his task. James Rothschild, who was a citizen of Napoleon's France at the time, arranged the transfer of this gold to Wellington, making an enormous profit on the

14

transaction while sealing the fate of Napoleon. The rest is His-story.

If the defeat of Napoleon isn't enough to convince you of the threat of bankers then there is also the warning given by President Thomas Jefferson:

> I believe that banking institutions are more dangerous to our liberties than standing armies. Already they have raised up a money aristocracy that has set the government at defiance. The issuing power should be taken from the banks and restored to the government to whom it properly belongs.

War and the New World Order

The power elites are trying to impose a "New World Order," where the power elites are in essence elevated to nobility and the rest of humanity is reduced to serfdom. This is not new at all but the same White Supremacy and Western Imperialism garbage that has been around for the past few centuries. But the biggest tragedy in this whole affair of trying to impose a "New World Order" is the extreme lack of human compassion on the part of the power elites. They are determined to impose their "New World Order" no matter how many people have to suffer or die. The power elites perceive human life only as another capital resource not much different than say a computer or a desk. To the power elites war is just one more device in their bag of tricks to manipulate people and make them more exploitable. There is no concern about the hundreds of millions of lives that are lost in worthless and fraudulent struggles. The Civil War, World War I & II, the Korean War, and the Vietnam War were all conflicts where the international power elites manipulated and exploited markets, public opinion, and certain well-placed individuals to guarantee that war would occur. War and the fear of war make people very vulnerable and they become easy prey to the will of the power elites. While the power elites are telling the people they are pursuing a path for peace, they are actually working to ensure war.

One prime example of where the international power elites lead by international bankers intervened to guarantee war in an effort to exploit the people is the U.S. Civil War. This point is illustrated by the First Chancellor of Germany, Otto von Bismarck. In 1876 he said:

> The division of the United States into federations of equal force was decided long before the Civil War by the high financial powers of Europe. These bankers were afraid that the United States, if they remained in one block and as one nation, would attain economic and financial domination over the world. The voice of the Rothschilds prevailed. They saw tremendous booty if they could substitute two feeble democracies, indebted to the financiers, for the vigorous Republic which was practically self-providing. Therefore, they started their emissaries in order to exploit the question of slavery and, thus, to dig an abyss between the two parts of the Republic...Lincoln's personality surprised them. His being a candidate had not troubled them; they thought to easily dupe a woodcutter. But Lincoln read their plots and understood that the South was not the worst foe, but the financiers.

During the early part of the Civil War the plot of the power elites seem to be working. The Union had lost most of the early battles and it seemed like a successful Confederate succession was just a matter of time.

In the midst of the war the National Banking Act of 1863 was passed, giving the international bankers more control of the U.S. economy. After passage of the Act, President Abraham Lincoln had this to say:

The money power preys upon the nation in times of peace and conspires against it in times of adversity. It is more despotic than monarchy, more selfish than bureaucracy. I see in the near future a crisis approaching that unnerves me and causes me to tremble for the safety of my country. Corporations have enthroned, an era of corruption in high places will follow, and the money power of the country will endeavor to prolong its reign by working upon the prejudices of the people until the wealth is aggregated in a few hands and the republic is destroyed.

Some might say that all this happened over 100 years ago, things are different now. But all one needs to do is open their eyes and look around, and they will discover that the money power's grasp upon this country and all the countries of the world is as tight as ever. Despite the warnings of presidents such as Thomas Jefferson and Abraham Lincoln, the U.S. to a large extent is controlled by a group of international power elites.

The passage of the Federal Reserve Act on December 23, 1913 which created the Federal Reserve System is what gave the international power elites its major inroad to dominate U.S. banking institutions and the U.S. economy. This act gives tremendous power to the Federal Reserve Banks which are not government agencies but private corporations owned by member banks which are in turn owned and controlled to a large extent by international banking houses.

In analyzing the Federal Reserve System one needs to ask oneself: Why is so much of what the Federal Reserve does a secret? The Federal Reserve is more secretive than either the Pentagon or the CIA. For example, the true or Class A stockholders of the Federal Reserve Banks is one of the most tightly held secrets in the world.

Poverty and the Power Elites

Another tragedy is that in the minds of these power elites it is also extremely desirable to have poor and hungry people in the world; poor and hungry people are very easy targets for exploitation. There is no need to appeal to their hearts and minds, they can be easily manipulated through their stomachs. Manipulation of the poor is one of the main reasons why the power elites give so much money away to charity (the Rockefeller Foundation, the Ford Foundation, the Carnegie Foundation, the Welfare System, etc.). It makes them look like the good guys in the eyes of the poor when in reality they are the main cause of their suffering. And when someone tries to explain that these people are not really helping by giving away all that money, it often falls on deaf ears.

Everyone needs to be aware that poverty and hunger is not so much a function of a scarcity of resources but more of a function of the need of rich to exploit poor people in order to maintain their wealth. Taking food as an example, there is more than enough food grown to feed everyone in the world but the poor just cannot afford it because food prices are too high. And if many of the farmers are so poor that they need a charity concert like Farm Aid to bail them out, then where could all the profits be going? Could it possibly be going to large multi-national agricultural corporations, such as ADM, "supermarket to the world?"

One prime example of the power elites manipulation of the poor and the working class is the fact that the union leaders who are suppose to represent the interests of union members but in reality represent the interests of the power elites. You find many union leaders are members of organizations that represent the interests of the power elites such as the Council on Foreign Relations or the Trilateral Commission. The union leaders' function, is like that of the leaders of underdeveloped nations, which is to provide a docile labor force at the cheapest price possible.

U.S. Policy and the New World Order

So where do Blacks stand in this "New World Order"? On the bottom, so what else is new. Though government officials claim they are trying to combat oppressing conditions, an examination of government policies will show a different story. Let's examine a few government policy examples that exist to ensure that Blacks remain at the bottom of American society.

If we examine the drug problem, we will find a great many politicians giving lip service about some "War on Drugs" but the situation doesn't seem to be getting any better. Now, why is that? I can tell you one major reason why the government's "War on Drugs" is not working, and that is because the government is one of the largest dealers and transporters of illegal drugs. As far back as 1948, there is ample evidence to show that the government provided military support for the drug smugglers of the Golden Triangle in Southeast Asia. And in 1986 Senator John Kerry (Dem. Mass.) implicated the CIA in illegal drug trafficking. Today, we also hear reports of police officers giving children drugs to sell for them. And this is just the tip of the iceberg. While we are depending on the government to reduce the flow of drugs into our communities, it is actually the government that is directly responsible for a good portion of the drugs on the street. We must realize that the government is not trying to stop the flow of drugs into the Black community, it is just too effective as a tool of oppression.

What about U.S. policy concerning AIDS? Given the dubious history of the United States Chemical and Biological Warfare (CBW) programs and the goals and methods of the international power elites, I have very little doubt that AIDS is a man-made phenomena. If the power elites have little to no sympathy for the millions who die in war then I am quite certain that they have no sympathy for the victims of AIDS, especially when the vast majority of the victims are homosexuals, IV drug users, and non-whites.

The U.S. government is also involved in a massive misinformation campaign about the cause of AIDS; AIDS is not caused by HIV (the "AIDS virus") alone but on any literature provided by the government or the medical establishment HIV is stated as the one and only cause of AIDS. The evidence that HIV is insufficient to cause AIDS is overwhelming, yet little of that evidence seems to make its way into the media Even Dr. Luc Montagnier, the French researcher who was the first to isolate HIV, now claims that HIV alone is insufficient to cause AIDS. And when it comes to misinformation about AIDS that is just the tip of the iceberg. Where are people being misinformed? Could it be that the government is not really interested in finding a cure?

The whole story would not be complete without looking at the U.S. government's attacks on organizations that oppose U.S. policy. The U.S. government has throughout its history brutally crushed or emasculated, mainly through illegal means, many organizations that have tried to improve the quality of life for Blacks such as the United Negro Improvement Association, Black Panther Party, Student Nonviolent Coordinating Committee, Revolutionary Action Movement, Nation of Islam, and Republic of New Afrika. Many of the members of these organizations were assassinated by law enforcement officials and many more were imprisoned on fraudulent charges. The government will go to almost any lengths to destroy any effective organization that opposes its policies.

Brave New World

We must realize that the power elites are deadly serious about seeing that any renovation of the international system of White Supremacy and Western Imperialism is in their interest. They use a variety of carrot and stick tactics to maintain political and economic control. Control techniques will be more vicious or less, depending on a combination of factors involving the state of the economy and, more importantly, the state of popular opposition. The more threatening and persistent the moves to counter their plans and build alternative models – the more violent will be their tactics of repression.

Watch out! Totalitarianism is coming fast to your neighborhood, no coupons necessary. But be careful! Because this new totalitarianism will be little different from the past because this time around it will be labeled "Democracy." Take note from Aldous Huxley's *Brave New World*:

> There is of course, no reason why the new totalitarianisms should resemble the old. Government by clubs and firing squads, by artificial famine, mass imprisonment and mass deportation, is not merely inhuman (nobody cares much about that nowadays); it is demonstrably inefficient and in the age of advanced technology, inefficiency is the sin against the Holy Ghost. A really efficient totalitarian state would be one in which the all-powerful executive of political bosses and their army of managers control a population of slaves who do not have to be coerced, because they love their servitude. To make them love it is the task assigned, in present-day totalitarian states, to ministries of propaganda, newspaper editors and school teachers...

As you read through the rest of this book, try to keep in mind that my purpose in writing this book is to give Black people a little insight into the tools of White Supremacy so that maybe in future struggles we will be better able to combat our true enemies. Knowledge is power and the better we understand the root causes of our oppression the more likely our good intentions will lead to freedom.

21

CHAPTER 2

FASCISM: U.S.A. STYLE

> The great masses of the people... will more easily fall victim to a big lie than a small one.
>
> Adolf Hitler
> Mein Kampf (My Battle)

I will admit that the accusation of deliberate global genocide is very serious but it is accusation that is well-founded based on a great deal of evidence from a wide range of sources. First let's look at some facts on the world situation today:

o Over 1 billion - about one in every five on earth - do not get enough food to lead fully productive lives. Yet there is more than enough food for everyone in the world. For example, if the 1986 harvest was distributed evenly if could support a population of 6 billion - the projected population of the earth in the year 1998. [For more information about the myth of food scarcity and how most of the hunger in the world is caused by the policies of western nations and multinational corporations see *Food First: Beyond the Myth of Scarcity* by Frances Moore Lappe and Joseph Collins.]

o Everyday at least 25,000 people die from their everyday use of water. Dirty water is both the world's greatest killer, and biggest single pollution problem. Diarrhea alone kills at least 4.6 million young children a year. In the so-called Third World countries, where the severity of this problem is the greatest, the biggest polluters of industrial waste are multinational corporation taking advantage of cheap wages.

o According to the World Health Organization (WHO), 30 million adults and 10 million children will be infected with the "AIDS" virus by the year 2000. WHO estimates that 10 million people will suffer full-blown AIDS by the turn of the century, 90% of them in developing countries. This estimate given in 1991 is a 33% increase over their last estimate, which the means the estimates will continue to increase. [As will be explained chapter 11, WHO is responsible for the AIDS pandemic in Africa, also see *London Times*, May 11, 1987, "Smallpox vaccine 'triggered AIDS virus.'"]

More Proof of Global Genocide

I will admit that these fact alone prove little if anything but it you take such facts and start to piece them with other information a definite pattern begins to develop. A pattern that has repeated itself many times throughout the course of human history. Let's take a look at some of this information:

o In Global Report 2000, a report commissioned by the Carter Administration, the need was stated to eliminate one billion people that report termed "excess population" and "useless eaters."

o The history of the U.S. chemical and biological warfare program and the increasing evidence that AIDS is a man-made phenomena.

o The past behavior of so-called Christian Europeans. In the century after the Spanish Conquistadores, led by Cortez, landed in Central and South America, the population was reduced by two-thirds; 20 million men, women and children perished. Of the 6 to 9 million Indians who originally lived in the Amazon rainforest, only about 200,000 now survive. There were 300,000 Aborigines in Australia when "The First Fleet" landed in Botany Bay; a century later 60,000 remained. Every single Carib Indian on the island of Hispaniola (Haiti/Dominican Republic) was killed or deported by Spanish colonialists, to be replaced by slaves from Africa. The people of the 600 Indian nations of North America were reduced by half to two-thirds by 1860. Over 100 million African were killed as a result of the Slave Trade which lasted over 350 years.

o The function and history of such organizations as the United Nations, International Monetary Fund, World Bank, Federal Reserve System, Trilateral Commission, Council on Foreign Relations, Carnegie Endowment for International Peace, Rockefeller Foundation, Ford Foundation.

o The illegal overthrown of legitimate government by the CIA and other U.S. government agencies.

o The severe political repression of individuals and organizations that oppose U.S. policy by government agencies.

o The doctrines and history of White Supremacy and Western Imperialism.

FEMA

Once you get past the surface explanations of these events, you would have to be a fool or someone unconcerned about their future and the

24

future of human beings in general to reject totally that is a definitive pattern developing. I hate to be an alarmists but the all the signs are there, you just have to wake up a recognize them. Remember the Jewish people in Nazi Germany didn't get formal invitations in the mail to be guests in concentration camps with deluxe sleeping accommodations in a gas chamber. They got kick out bed in the middle of the night, no RSVP necessary. When listening to the clamming voices our so-called "Negro" leaders, we must remember that there were also a few Jewish people who to the very end proclaim that soon this will all be over and things will get back to normal. For the Jewish people in Nazi Germany there were definitely many foretelling signs and events that warned that such a thing as the extermination of 6 million of them was indeed possible and very likely.

For those of you who refuse to believe that such things are not possible in the United States of America, let's look at some more facts:

o Fascism is on the rise in the U.S. but this time around they are calling patriotism. Just try burning a flag.

o Executive Order 9066 signed by President Roosevelt on February 19, 1942 allowed over 100,000 American citizens of Japanese ancestry to send to concentration camps.

o In 1976 President Ford ordered the Federal Emergency Preparedness Agency (FEPA) to develop plans to establish government control of the mechanisms of productions and distribution, of energy sources, wages and salaries, credit and the flow of money in American financial institutions in any (heretofore undefined) "national emergency." This Executive Order (EO 11921) also indicated that, when a state of emergency is declared by the President, Congress could not review the matter for a period of six months.

o President Carter, in 1977, signed Executive Order 12148 which created the Federal Emergency Management Agency (FEMA) to replace FEPA. This Presidential Directive mandated an interface between the Department of Defense (DOD) and FEMA for civil defense planning and funding.

o When Ronald Reagan came to power he gave FEMA vastly expanded executive emergency powers and appointed retired National Guard General Louis O. Giuffrida as his "emergency czar." In 1970, Giuffrida had written a paper at the Army War College in Carlisle, Pa., in which he advocated martial law in case of a national uprising by "militant negroes." The paper also advocated the roundup and transfer to "assembly centers or relocation camps" of at least 21 million "American Negroes."

o In 1984, 10 huge prison camps were "activated" by a highly classified National Security Decision Directive (NSDD) signed by President Reagan. Sites of the prison facilities include Eglin Air Force Base, Florida; Vandenberg AFB, California; Fort McCoy, Wisconsin; Fort Benning, Georgia; Fort Huachuca, Arizona; Fort Chaffe, Arkansas; Fort Drum, New York; Fort Indian Gap, Pennsylvania; and Camp A.P. Hill, Virginia.

o In April 1984, in a combined exercise, labeled Rex-84 Bravo, FEMA and DOD led other federal agencies and departments, including the Central Intelligence Agency, the Secret Service, the Treasury, the Federal Bureau of Investigation, and the Veterans Administration through a gaming exercise to test military assistance in case of a "national emergency."

I hope these little bits of fact has made it quite clear that the United States of America ("home of the free") is just one Presidential Decree away from being a dictatorship. The only thing necessary for this to occur is a "national emergency." Maybe an AIDS epidemic might qualify or better yet a Drug Crisis. Sounds quite Hegelian to me. In the words of Arsenio: "These aren't jokes mind you, just some thoughts that make you go 'Mmmmm.'"

Reagan, Bush and the Nazis

I know, I know. There's still a few of you with your yellow ribbons, desert storm tee-shirts, and your Colin "Cut It Off And Kill It" Powell or Norman "Bombs Over Baghdad" Schwartzkopf for President buttons who still aren't convince, so let's dig a little deeper. On May 5, 1985, Ronald Reagan visited Bitburg cemetery in Germany where 2,500 German soldiers are buried, 49 of them SS men. In the speech he gave at the cemetery he characterized the Nazi Waffen SS as "victims." For average folks this doesn't mean a whole hell of a lot but for those young, impressionable Neo-Nazis, stuff like this is simply orgasmic. I heard there was one small town in Idaho that had a problem with sticky floors for a weeks.

Less than two weeks later, on May 17, Ronald Reagan was the keynote speaker at the Shoreham Hotel for 400 luncheon guests. The luncheon was a Republican Party affair and the 400 guests were part of a special outreach unit, the National Republican Heritage Groups Council (RHGC).

The RHGC is an umbrella for various ethic Republican clubs and operates under the auspices of the Republican National Committee. It has a special type of outreach and appears to have consciously recruited some of its members and some of its leaders from an Eastern European emigre network which includes anti-Semites, racists, authoritarians, and fascists, including sympathizers and collaborators of Hitler's Third Reich, former Nazis, and even possible war criminals. The persons in this network are a part of the radical right faction of the ethic communities they claim to represent.

Some of the persons present at the 1985 luncheon would later join the 1988 election campaign of President George Bush. It is from this group that Bush presidential campaign assembled its ethic outreach unit in 1988 - a unit that saw eight resignations by persons charged with anti-Semitism, racism, and even Nazi collaboration.

Who are some of these "friendly" representatives from the RHGC, well let's find out:

o Laszlo Pasztor: The founding chair and a key figure in the Council, Pasztor began his political career in the Hungarian pro-Nazi party and served in Berlin at the end of World War II. He continues to be involved in ultra-rightist groups and fascist networks while working with the GOP.

o Radi Slavoff: The RHGC's executive director is a member of a Bulgarian fascist group and leader of the Bulgarian GOP unit of the Council. He was able to get the leader of his Bulgarian nationalist group an invitation to the White House even though that leader was being investigated for concealing alleged World War II war crimes.

o Nicolas Nazarenko: A former World War II officer in the German SS Cossack Division, Nazarenko heads the Cossack GOP unit in the RHGC and had declared that Jews are his "ideological enemy." He is still active with pro-Nazi elements in the U.S.

To confirm how important the Republican Party felt that the National Republican Heritage Groups Council, President Reagan told the 1985 meeting:

The work of all of you has meant a very great deal to me personally, to the Party, and to our cause.... I can't think of any others who have made a more vital contribution to the effort than those of you who are in this room today.... I want to encourage you to keep building the Party. Believe me, bringing more ethnic

Americans into the fold is the key to the positive realignment that we are beginning to see take shape.

For those of you still not convince, let's dig even deeper. Let's take a look at Prescott Bush, the investment banking father of George Bush. Prescott Sheldon Bush was a partner in the investment banking firm of Brown Brothers, Harriman & Co. Prescott Bush was also a member of the Skull and Bones, class of 1917. The Skull and Bones is an elite secret society open only to a select 15 males in their senior year at Yale University. George Bush is also a Bonesman, class of 1948.

Prescott Bush was one of the directors of the Union Banking Corporation of New York City. The Union Banking Corporation was a joint Thyssen-Harriman banking operation. Fritz Thyssen was a German steel magnate and a financial backer of Adolf Hitler. In 1932 the Union Banking Corporation had the following directors:

o E. Roland Harriman: Vice President of W.A. Harriman & Co., New York. Bonesman, 1917.
o H.J. Kouwenhoven: Nazi banker, managing partner of August Thyssen Bank and Bank voor Handel en Scheepvaart N.V. (one of the bank that transfer funds to Hitler). Nazi.
o Knight Wooley: Director of Guaranty Trust, New York and Director of the Federal Reserve Bank of N.Y. Bonesman, 1917.
o Cornelius Lievense: President, Union Banking Corp. and Director of Holland-American Investment Corp.
o Ellery Sedgewick James: Partner, Brown Brothers & Co., New York. Bonesman, 1917.
o Johann Groninger: Director of Bank voor Handel en Scheepvaart and Vereninigte Stahlwerke (Thyssen's steel operations). Nazi.
o J.L. Guinter: Director Union Banking Corp.
o Prescott Sheldon Bush: Partner, Brown Brothers, Harriman. Bonesman, 1917.

Out of the eight directors of the Union Banking Corp., six are either Nazis or Bonesmen from the class of 1917. Mmmmmmmm. And the list of Nazi collaboration before and during World War II goes on. There is evidence to support that the Ford Motor Company, Standard Oil of New Jersey (Exxon), Chase Bank and the Federal Reserve Bank of New York, all had ties to and supported Nazi Germany before and during World War II. Looks like contrary to the conventional wisdom that Nazism was and is very popular among the power elites in the United States.

CHAPTER 3

THE WAYS OF THE TYRANT

> Tyranny, like hell, is not easily conquered; yet we have this consolation with us, that the harder the conflict, the more glorious the triumph. What we obtain too cheap, we esteem too lightly; 'tis dearness only that gives everything its value. Heaven knows how to put a proper price upon its goods; and it would be strange indeed, if so celestial an article as Freedom should not be highly rated.
>
> Thomas Paine

Recalling the CIA's assassination plot on Patrice Lumumba, if you read the *Soliloquy of Patrice Lumumba* and understand the goals and methods of white supremacy and western imperialism, you will realize why the power elites wanted him dead:

> For a thousand years you, African, suffered like a beast, your ashes strewn to the wind that roams the desert. Your tyrants built the lustrous, magic temples to preserve your soul, preserve your suffering. Barbaric right of fist and the whiteman's right to whip, you had the right to die, you also could weep.
> In your totem they carved endless hunger, endless bonds, and even in the cover of the woods a ghastly cruel death was watching,

snaky, crawling to you like branches from the holes and heads of trees, embraced your body and your ailing soul. Then they put a treacherous big viper on your chest: on your neck they laid the yoke of fire-water, they took your sweet wife for glitter of cheap pearls, your incredible riches that nobody could measure. From your hut, the tom-toms sounded into dark of night carrying cruel laments up mighty black rivers about abused girls, streams of tears and blood, about ships that sailed to country where the little man wallows in an ant-hill and where a dollar is king, to that damned land which they called a motherland. There your child, your wife were ground, day and night by frightful, merciless mill, crushing them dreadful pain. You are men like others. They preach you to believe that good white god will reconcile all men at last. By fire you grieved and sang the moaning songs of homeless beggar that sinks at stranger's doors.

And when a craze possessed you and your blood boiled through the night, you danced, you moaned, obsessed by father's passion. Like fury of a storm to lyrics of a manly tune, a strength burst out of you for a thousand years of misery in metallic voice of jazz, in uncovered outcry that thunders through the continent in gigantic surf. The whole world surprised, woke up in panic to the violent rhythm of blood, to violent rhythm of jazz, the white man turning pallid over this new song that carries torch of purple through the dark of night.

The dawn is here, my brother, dawn! Look in our faces, a new morning in our old Africa. Ours only will now be the land, the water, mighty rivers poor African was surrendering for a thousand years. And hard torches of the sun will shine for us again. They'll dry the tears in eyes and spittle on your face. The moment when you break the chains, the heavy fetters, the evil, cruel and gallant Congo will

arise from black soil, a free and gallant
Congo - the black blossom, the black seed!

Lumumba was a strong African leader that refuse to
subjugate himself or his people to Western
imperialism, which to the power elites is a crime
punishable by death.

The Death of Patrice Lumumba

From John Stockwell, former Chief Angola Task
Force and the highest ranking CIA Official to go
public, we learn just how determined the U.S.
government was to eliminate Lumumba. In his *In
Search of Enemies: A CIA Story*, Stockwell states:

> The former deputy director of plans
> (operations), Richard Bissell, testified that
> feasibility studies of how to assassinate Patrice
> Lumumba had been made in 1961. Sid Gottlieb,
> the CIA chief of the Office of Technical Services
> had hand-carried poison to Kinshasa for the
> Lumumba operation. Gottlieb himself testified
> that years later, the CIA director Richard
> Helms, had ordered him to destroy all records
> of the tests he had run of specific poisons to
> be used in killing Lumumba....
> In the Lumumba assassination plot the CIA
> was particularly diligent in its planning. Sid
> Gottlieb, chief of Technical Services Division,
> and courier of the poison, had no sooner
> reached Kinshasa than headquarters had
> followed him with cables urging that the poison
> be given to Lumumba promptly, before its
> power diminished. An agent was located who
> agreed to administer the fatal dose. A CIA staff
> officer on the one hand refused to do the
> killing, but on the other did agree to lure
> Lumumba into a situation where he could be
> poisoned. The poison was not used, apparently
> because of difficulties in staging the killing,
> but a month later, on January 17, 1961,

Lumumba was beaten by henchmen of Congolese politicians who had close relationships with the CIA.

CIA complicity is further demonstrated by John Stockwell's encounter with a CIA Official who opened up to him and described his "adventure in Lubumbashi, driving about town after curfew with Patrice Lumumba's body in the trunk of his car, trying to decide what to do with it."

Neocolonialism

The Patrice Lumumba assassination plot is not isolated incidence but rather standard operational procedure for the U.S. government. In the wake of World War II, old-style colonialism gave way to neocolonialism. The neocolonial state has formal independence but as Kwame Nkrumah put it: "in reality its economic system and thus its political policy is directed from outside." Instead of a single master, the neocolonial state has many new masters: e.g., Western governments (especially the U.S.), the International Monetary Fund, the World Bank, banking consortia, and global corporations.

The U.S. makes it a habit to intervene, to sabotage and to smash governments which challenge the tightly woven fabric of dependency:

1898-1902	occupation of Cuba
1899-1902	Philippines
1901	"acquires" Puerto Rico
1906-09	occupation of Cuba
1909	Nicaragua, overthrow of Zelaya
1912-25	occupation of Nicaragua
1914	Mexico
1914-34	occupation of Haiti
1916-24	occupation of Dominican Republic
1917-23	occupation of Cuba
1919	occupation of Honduran ports
1926-33	occupation of Nicaragua
1947-49	Greece

1953	Iran, overthrow of Mossadeq
1954	Guatemala, overthrow of Arbenz
1958	Lebanon
1960-61	Congo (now Zaire), overthrow of Lumumba
1961	Bay of Pigs invasion of Cuba
1961-75	Vietnam, Laos, Cambodia
1964	Brazil, overthrow of Goulart
1964	Indonesia
1965-66	occupation of Dominican Republic
1966	Ghana, overthrow of Nkrumah
1970	Bolivia
1973	Chile, overthrow of Allende
1974-76	Angola
1979	El Salvador
1980	Nicaragua
1983	occupation of Grenada
1985	Cambodia
1986	Angola
1989	Panama
1990-91	Iraq

Debt dependency is one of the neocolonial leashes around the so-called Third World countries' neck. The leash is let out to allow Western-directed development projects to gallop ahead - returning enormous profits to foreign corporations and banks. Or, the debt leash can be pulled in tight - as part of an economic and political destabilization campaign - to strangle a rebellious nation into submission.

Destabilization is the dominant system's "cure" for any government which threatens the economic freedom of international business as it becomes "more" responsive to the needs of its people. And the global doctors know how painful their cure can be; it kills the body to save the cancer. The overthrow of Chile's democratically elected government is a case in point.

The Overthrow of Allende

The case of Chile's destabilization following Salvador Allende's presidential victory is well documented. Nixon, Kissinger, and CIA director Richard Helms succeeded in their efforts to "make the economy scream" by orchestrating an economic blockade of the country - cutting off U.S. aid and all lines of international public and private bank finance and orchestrating economic and political sabotage within the country. Military assistance, however, was increased in order to encourage and enable the army to overthrow Allende's government and smash Chilean democracy to bring back "economic freedom."

More than 30,000 people were killed, including President Allende, resisting the military coup of September 11, 1973. Since then, over 2,000 people have "disappeared" and most are presumed dead. More than 100,000 people have been jailed for political reasons; torture is commonplace. Thousands of people have been forced to flee into exile.

Today hunger and starvation have been replaced the community-based nutrition and food programs of the Allende government. Out of a sample of 19,000 children in a Church-sponsored study two-thirds were found to be malnourished in 1976. Infant mortality, reduced during the Allende years, jumped 18 percent during the first year of military rule. Before the coup unemployment had been reduced to 3.1 percent. By 1976 about one-fourth of the population had no income. A 1976 IMF study reveals the extent of income redistribution - from the poor to the rich - since the coup. In 1972, 63 percent of the total national income went to wage and salaried workers while property owners received 37 percent in the form of profits, dividends, and rent. By 1974, 62 percent went to the propertied sector and labor's share was cut to 38 percent.

The Intervention Racket

From Major General Smedley D. Butler, two-time winner of the Congressional Medal of Honor, we get a first-hand account of the intervention racket of the U.S. government. In an article, "America's Armed Forces" by John Lamperti and first printed in *Common Sense* (October 1935), General Smedley is quoted as saying:

> War is a racket.... It may seem odd for me, a military man, to adopt such a comparison. Truthfulness compels me to. I spent 33 years and 4 months in active service as a member of our country's most agile military force - the Marine Corps.... And during the period I spent most of my time being a high-class muscle man for Big Business, for Wall Street and for the bankers. In short, I was a racketeer for capitalism....
>
> Thus I helped make Mexico and especially Tampico safe for American oil interests in 1914. I helped make Haiti and Cuba a decent place for the National City Bank [Citibank] boys to collect revenues in. I helped in the raping of half a dozen Central American republics for the benefit of Wall Street.... I helped purify Nicaragua for the international banking house of Brown Brothers in 1909-1912. I brought light to the Dominican Republic for American sugar interests in 1916. I helped make Honduras 'right' for American fruit companies in 1903....
>
> Looking back on it, I feel I might have given Al Capone a few hints. The best *he* could do was to operate his racket in three city districts. We Marines operated on three *continents*. [Emphasis original.]

CHAPTER 4

THE FED AND THE EATEN

> Experience declares that man is the only
> animal which devours his own kind; for
> I can apply no milder term to the
> governments of Europe, and to the
> general prey of the rich on the poor.
>
> Thomas Jefferson

On December 23, 1913, the Federal Reserve Act
created the Federal Reserve System (the Fed) which
is the central bank of the United States. The Fed's
stated principal function is to set monetary policy.
It uses three tools to control and regulate U.S.
money: reserve requirements (the percentage of
deposits that member banks [about 5,500 banks]
must set aside and not use for loans); discount rate
(the interest rate at which depository institutions
can borrow from the Reserve Banks); and open
market operations (the purchase and sale of
government securities).

Okay, that is the textbook explanation of the
Fed's function, but what I would like to explain is
the real function of the Fed: It's a racket! Forget
illegal drugs, forget illegal gambling the "boys" that
control the Federal Reserve System make Al Capone
look like Mother Teresa. Congressman Charles A.
Lindbergh of Minnesota, father of the famous flyer,
summed it up best when speaking on the House floor

38

on December 23, 1913, the day the Federal Reserve Act became law, Lindbergh said:

> This act establishes the most gigantic trust on earth. When the President [Wilson] signs this bill the invisible government of the Monetary Power will be legalized. ...the worst legislative crime of the age is perpetrated by this banking and currency bill.

THE DECEPTION

To prove to you that the Fed is a racket, the first thing I would like you to do is to take out a dollar bill. What does it say on the front at the very top? It says: Federal Reserve Note. That's right the Fed prints the money. And contrary to the conventional wisdom, the Fed is not part of the government but a private corporation. It is private corporation owned by international bankers and other money powers (more about ownership of the Fed later), many of whom are based in Europe. These money powers make tremendous profits by printing U.S. currency, and by buying and selling U.S. government securities. The profits obtain by these money powers is basically money stolen from average folks like you and me. The way the money is stolen is so devious and so interwoven in the fabric of modern society that very few people are even aware that the money is being stolen. And even fewer people are able to begin to comprehend this sinister plot.

TOTAL MONEY-MAKING MACHINE

I am sure everyone is familiar with the saying: Money doesn't grow on trees. While it is true that money doesn't grow on trees, it is quite possible to create money out of thin air or more precisely just by writing a check. This is exactly what you do when you write a check but don't have enough money in your account to cover the check. As long as you are able to put the money into your account before the check clears, everything is okay. But for those 2-3 days between when you write the check and when the check actually clears, you actually created money out of thin air for those few days. But what happens when the Fed writes a check? Former U.S. Representative Wright Patman, House Banking and Currency Committee, explains:

> Where does the Federal Reserve get the money with which to create bank reserves? Answer: It doesn't get the money, it creates it. When the Federal Reserve writes a check for a government bond it does exactly what any bank does, it creates money...it created money purely and simply by writing a check. And the recipient of the check wants cash, then the Federal Reserve can oblige him by printing the cash - Federal Reserve Notes - which the check receiver's commercial bank can hand over to him. *The Federal Reserve, in short, is a total money-making machine.* [Emphasis mine.]

INFLATION AND TAXES

The tools of this system of massive plunder are inflation and taxes. Inflation is the tool used to steal your money and taxes is the tool used to hide the fact that your money is being stolen. What I am about to say most people will simply refuse to believe and others may be shock by it but the Federal Reserve System is basically a sophisticated and legal counterfeit currency operation. The almighty dollar in reality has no real worth, it is only a promise by the U.S. government to pay debts. Everyone is familiar with the way a counterfeiter introduces money into the economy, free of charge (not including such things as the costs of paper, ink, presses, etc.). The Federal Reserve System works in the same manner, except that it is cloaked in economic "voodoo." The introduction of the addition money into the economy cause inflation - more money chasing the same amount of goods and services, hence, prices go up. Inflation is basically the theft of the wealth of the people by the money powers that control the government and Fed.

Taxes are use to hide the treachery and theft of this set-up. This fact is supported by a former Congressman Ron Paul from Texas:

> Strictly speaking, it probably is not "necessary" for the federal government to tax anyone directly. It could simply print the money it needs. However, that would be obvious to all what kind of counterfeiting operation the government is running. The present system combining taxation and inflation is akin to watering the milk: too much water and the people catch on.

And if the words of a former congressman is not enough to convince you, then what about the words of the "father of modern economics," John Maynard Keynes. Keynes theories form the basis of most economies of Western-industrial nations, including the United States. In 1919, in the book that would give him international prominence, *The Economic Consequences of the Peace*, Keynes states:

> Lenin was certainly right, there is no more surer, more subtler means of destroying the existing basis of society than to debauch the currency. By a continuing process of inflation, governments can confiscate secretly and unobserved, an important part of the wealth of the citizens. The process engages all the hidden forces of economics on the side of destruction and does it in a manner that not one man in a million can diagnose.... If governments should refrain from regulation [taxation] and allowed matters to take their course [price explosion], the worthlessness of the money becomes

apparent and the fraud upon the public can be concealed no longer.

WHO OWNS THE FED

The Fed is a private corporation whose stockholders are member banks, many of which are controlled by international banking houses. The U.S. government owns absolutely no stock in the Federal Reserve. This fact was verified by a court case, Lewis v. United States, No. 80-5905, United States Court of Appeals, Ninth Circuit, 19 April 1982. The plaintiff, John L. Lewis, was injured by a vehicle owned and operated by a federal reserve bank and brought action alleging jurisdiction under the Federal Tort Claims Act. The United States District Court for the Central District of California, David W. Williams, Jr., dismissed the case holding that federal reserve banks were not federal agencies within the meaning of the Act and the court therefore lacked subject-matter jurisdiction. An appeal was taken. The Court of Appeals, Poole, Circuit Judge, held that federal reserve banks are not federal instrumentalities for purposes of the Act, but are independent, privately owned and locally controlled corporations.

The real owners of the Federal Reserve is one of the best kept secrets in the world because of a proviso on passage of the Federal Reserve Act. It was agreed that no information would be released on the Class A stockholders of Federal Reserve Banks. But, R.E. McMaster, a publisher of a newsletter, *The Reaper*, asked his Swiss and Saudi Arabian contacts which banks hold controlling interest in the Federal Reserve Bank of New York and this was their reply:

Owner number one, Rothschild Banks of London and Berlin; Owner number two, Lazard Brothers Banks of Paris; Owner number three, Israel Moses Seif Banks of Italy; Owner number four, Warburg Bank of Hamburg and Amsterdam; Owner number five, Lehman Brothers Bank of

New York; Owner number six, Kuhn, Loeb Bank of New York; Owner number seven, Chase Manhattan Bank of New York; Owner number eight, Goldman Sachs Bank of New York.

When you trace ownership down to the individual level, there are approximately 300 people, all known to each other and sometimes related to each other, who hold stock or shares in the Federal Reserve System. They comprise an interlocking, international banking cartel of wealth beyond comprehension.

THE FED AND THE U.S. GOVERNMENT

The relationship between the Fed and the government is a very complex one; but what it boils down to is that the Fed controls the government, as oppose to the government controlling the Fed. This point is reflected by the statement of Louis T. McFadden, Chairman, Banking and Currency Committee, United States Congress when in 1933 he said:

> Every effort has been made by the Fed to conceal its powers but the truth is - the Fed has usurped the government. It controls everything here [in Congress] and it controls all our foreign relations. It makes and breaks governments at will.

One measure of the Fed's awesome power is that about two-thirds of all deposits in the U.S. ($1.5 quadrillion) are in Federal Reserve member banks.

THE CREATION OF THE FED

An examination of how the Fed was created will reveal that the Fed was designed by international money powers to ensure that they would be able to dominate the U.S. economy. As far back as the Civil War and even earlier these money powers were intervening in the domestic affairs of the United States in order that they would be able to dominate the economy of the United States like they were able to dominate the economies of Europe.

Let's start at around the turn of the twentieth century. There is no central bank in the United States despite the best efforts of the power elites but this was soon to change. In attempt to undermine the public trust of the current banking system two panics (one in 1893 and another one in 1907) were deliberately staged, primarily by the efforts of J.P. Morgan. An article published in Life magazine by historian Frederick L. Allen in April 1949 reviewed this plot. In the article, "Did Morgan Precipitate the Panic?" the following was written:

> Oakleigh Thorne, the president of that particular trust company, testified later before a congressional committee that his bank had been subjected to only moderate withdrawals...that he had not applied for help, and that it was the [Morgan] "sore point" statement alone that had caused the run on the bank. From this testimony, plus the disciplinary measures taken by the Clearing House against the Heinze, Morse and Thomas banks, plus other fragments of supposedly pertinent evidence, certain chroniclers have arrived at the ingenious conclusion that the Morgan interests took advantage of the unsettled conditions during the Autumn of 1907 to precipitate the panic, guiding it shrewdly as it progressed so that it would kill off rival banks and consolidate the preeminence of the banks within the Morgan orbit.

It should also be taken into account that in both panics J.P. Morgan "saved Wall Street" while making enormous profits in the process.

In February 1895, Morgan sold $65 million dollars worth of gold to the government in return for bonds worth 104 1/2, then quickly disposed of them in the market at 112 1/4. The deal was

44

arranged to stop the "endless chain" outflow of Treasury gold that was already far below the level required to back the currency in circulation.

Then, on November 4, 1907 at midnight, with the New York City's biggest banks beset by runs that had gone on for three weeks, Morgan locked the trust presidents into the West Room of his 36th Street office. By 5 a.m., they pledged $25 million to salvage the banks and Morgan brought Tennessee Coal and Iron, whose dying owner was about to "tear Wall Street down" by declaring bankruptcy. Morgan's panic tactics were so successful that by 1909 his disclosed resources were $2 billion but his real wealth was much greater. Through interlocking directorships, his company controlled or influenced more than 100 of the nation's top corporations and banks with total assets well above $20 billion.

These two panics were planned in order to send a clear message throughout the U.S., and that message was that a central bank was necessary to prevent future instability in the banking industry. In 1907 Senator Nelson W. Aldrich (maternal grandfather to the Rockefeller brothers) declared, "Something has got to be done. We may not always have Pierpont Morgan with us to meet a banking crisis." And in 1908 Congress established the National Monetary Commission to examine the question of changes to the banking system and named a number of representatives of the international banking establishment to it. They included Paul Warburg, Senator Aldrich, and "Colonel" Edward M. House. After two years touring Europe at taxpayers' expense, the members of the committee held a secret meeting in Jekyll Island, Georgia, at the Jekyll Island Hunt Club (owned by J.P. Morgan). One of the attendees, Frank Vanderlip, President of Kuhn-Loeb's National City Bank of New York, wrote in 1935 about this meeting:

Despite my views about the value to society of greater publicity for the affairs of corporations, there was an occasion, near the close of 1910, when I was secretive - indeed as furtive - as any conspirator. I do not feel it is any exaggeration to speak of our secret expedition to Jekyll Island as the occasion of the actual conception of what eventually became the Federal Reserve System.... Discovery, we knew, simply must not happen, or else all our time and effort would be wasted.

When the recommendations from the National Monetary Commission were presented to Congress as the Aldrich Bill, it was defeated in 1911. Part of the reason was the guarantee of a Presidential veto by President William H. Taft. In light of this roadblock the money powers went to work on the 1912 Presidential Election. In *America's 60 Families*, Ferninand Lundberg describes what happened:

As soon as [Theodore] Roosevelt signified that he would again challenge Taft (on the ticket of the Progressive "Bull Moose" Party) the President's defeat was inevitable. Throughout the three-cornered fight [Taft-Roosevelt-Woodrow Wilson (who supported the Aldrich Bill)] Roosevelt had [Morgan agents] Munsey and Perkins constantly at his heels, supplying money, going over speeches, bringing people from Wall Street in to help, and, in general, carrying the entire burden of the campaign against Taft.... Perkins and J.P. Morgan and Company were the substance of the Progressive Party; everything else was trimming.... In short, most of Roosevelt's campaign was supplied by the two Morgan hatchet men who were seeking Taft's scalp.

Wilson was elected President with 41 percent of the popular vote. The Aldrich Bill was resubmitted as the Federal Reserve Act and voted into law on December 23, 1913. With the establishment of the Federal Reserve System the international banking establishment had finally triumphed, the U.S. now had a central bank.

Colonel Ely Garrison further corroborates that the idea for both the Aldrich Bill and the Federal Reserve Act had originated in the large international banking houses of Europe. Garrison was a friend and financial advisor to both President Theodore Roosevelt and President Woodrow Wilson. In his autobiographical book, *Roosevelt, Wilson and the Federal Reserve Act*, Garrison wrote:

> Mr. Paul Warburg is the man who got the Federal Reserve Act together after the Aldrich Plan aroused such nation-wide resentment and opposition. The mastermind of both plans was Alfred Rothschild of London.

Paul Moritz Warburg, whom President Wilson subsequently appointed first Chairman of the Federal Reserve Board of Governors, was an immigrant from Germany. His primary allegiance was not to the United States but to his family banking house of M.M. Warburg Company of Hamburg and Amsterdam.

During World War I, the M. M. Warburg Company financed Germany's war against the Allied forces. Paul's brother, Max, headed the German Secret Service. Also during the war years, Paul Warburg's firm of Kuhn, Loeb Company had five representatives in the United States Treasury Department in charge of Liberty Loans, thus financing America's war effort against the Kaiser. It is unlikely that noble considerations such as humanitarianism or patriotism inspired such interlocking international financing of the war.

CHAPTER 5

WAR! WHAT IS IT GOOD FOR?

> When the tyrant has disposed of foreign enemies by conquest or treaty, and there is nothing to fear from them, then he is always stirring up some war or other, in order that the people may require a leader.
>
> Plato

"In governing the populace, unrest cannot be averted. Therefore, it must be channeled and cultivated." This is the creed of Big Brother, fictional dictator in George Orwell's 1984. To channel this unrest that cannot be averted, the world is divided into three Regional Governments (Oceania [the Americas, Great Britain, Australia, and South Africa], Eastasia [China, Japan, Mongolia, and Southeast Asia], and Eurasia [Russia, Europe, and Siberia]), three Superpowers that exist in a state of permanent war with each other in varying combinations. To "channel the unrest," Oceania sometimes is allied with Eastasia against Eurasia. Sometimes Oceania is allied with Eurasia against Eastasia. Sometimes Eurasia and Eastasia find a common enemy in Oceania. And so on. Thus, by maintaining permanent war, the unrest of the populace is channeled (loyalty, patriotism, moral equivalent to war [e.g., "War on Poverty," "War on

Crime," "War on Drugs"], etc.). To cultivate unrest, each superpower is governed by four ministries; a Ministry of Peace which conducts war; a Ministry of Plenty which regulates the manufacture and distribution of goods; a Ministry of Love which directs espionage, terror and hate; and a Ministry of Truth which keeps "truth" up to date. Over all stands Big Brother who sees all, knows all, who must be loved by all while everybody must hate everybody else.

The Foundations of Regional Governments

Norman Dodd, former Director, Committee to Investigate Tax Exempt Foundations, U.S. House of Representatives, in a testimony to the Illinois Joint Legislative Committee on Regional Government revealed to the committee the objectives of the Ford Foundation and the Carnegie Endowment for International Peace. On September 26, 1978, Dodd said the following about a conversion he had in 1953 with Roman Gaither, the President of the Ford Foundation:

...Mr. Gaither volunteered the following information and these are practically in his exact words.
"Mr. Dodd, we operate here under directives which emanate from the White House. Would you like to know what the substance of these directives is?"
I said, "Indeed I would Mr. Gaither."
Whereupon he then said the following, "We here operate and control our grant making policies in harmony with directives the substance of which is as follows: We shall use our grant making power so as to alter life in the United States that it can be comfortably merged with the Soviet Union."

Also in this same testimony, Mr. Dodd shares his experience at the office of the President of the Carnegie Endowment for International Peace:

> On arrival at the office of the President, I was greeted with this statement, "Mr. Dodd, we received your letter. We can answer all the questions but it will be a great deal of trouble. The reason it will be a great deal of trouble is because, with the ratification by the Senate of the United States of the United Nations Treaty, our job was finished. So we bundled all our records up, spanning roughly speaking 50 years, and put them in the warehouse.

Dodd goes on to tell how a member of his staff spent two weeks in this warehouse spot reading the minutes of this organization. He then continues his testimony:

> Now we are back in the period of 1908 and these minutes reported the following: The trustees of the Carnegie Endowment bring up a single question, namely if it desirable to alter the life of an entire people, is there any means more efficient than war to getting that end and they discussed this question at a very high academic and scholarly level for a year and they came up with an answer. There is no means more efficient than war, assuming the objective is altering the life of an entire people. That leads them to a question. How do we involve United States in a war....
> ...the trustees then answered the question of how to involve us in a war by saying we must control the diplomatic machinery of the United States. That brings up the question of how to secure that control and the answer is: We must control the State Department.
> ...the trustees turn their attention then to seeing to it that life does not revert in this country to what it was prior to 1914 and they hit upon the idea that in order to prevent that

reversion they must control education in this country. They realize that that is a very tremendous, really stupendous and complex task, much too great for them alone. So they approach the Rockefeller Foundation with the suggestion that the task be divided between the two of them.

The Capitalist Creation of Communism

For those who find it hard to believe the goal of the power elites is to merge the United States and Soviet Union, let's review a little history. The Bolshevik conquest of Imperial and Christian Russia was financed by international bankers. M. M. Warburg of Germany made millions available to Lenin and his band of revolutionaries, and arranged for their safe passage into Russia. In New York City Jacob Schiff, partner and brother-in-law of Warburg, contributed a known $20 million. Leon Trotsky, living in luxury with an excellent apartment, rent paid three months in advance, traveling in a chauffeured limousine, suddenly was given $10,000 pocket money, and an American passport supplied by the intervention of Woodrow Wilson. He traveled to Canada, then to Russia to join Lenin, openly declaring his determination to "carry forward" the revolution.

International bankers then proceeded to develop Communist Russia into a Superpower. From 1919 onward, each time the Communist dictatorship was about to fail, aid was rushed to Lenin, Stalin, Khrushchev, Brezhnev, or Gorbachev, from the West, especially from the United States. It might be said that World War I was fought to create a Communist State, and World War II was fought to expand that Communist State into a Superpower and a Regional World Government.

US Companies Support USSR During War

As an example of how Monopoly Capitalism promoted International Communism - an example which is pertinent because it concerns oil as does the recent crisis in the Middle East - the following article appeared in The Washington Observer of September 15, 1974:

> During the Korean War and the recent Vietnam War, Soviet Russia, whose oil fields except for a few very minor ones on Sakhalin Island, are too remote, was unable to supply the Communist satellite countries in the Far East across more than 2,000 miles of ocean. So the Soviets went shopping on the international oil market and made a deal with the world oil cartel to provide most of the liquid fuels for the Communist war machines in Korea and Vietnam. To supply the oil, the Rockefeller interests used mainly the Arabian-American Oil Company (ARAMCO), which is jointly owned by Standard Oil of California (30%), Texaco (30%), Standard Oil of New Jersey [Exxon] (30%), and Socony Vacuun (10%).

This occurred while the United States and Communist countries were at war against each other: U.S. companies helping to kill American soldiers by supplying the fuel for the Communist war machine.

War in the Gulf

To further demonstrate the use of war to achieve the goals of the International Power Elites, let's examine the events leading up to the recent war between the "Allies" and Iraq. Let's go back to the Islamic Revolution in Iran and the overthrow of the Shah, which is also around the time when Saddam Hussein formally replaced his older cousin General Ahmed Hassan al-Bakr as President of Iraq. Also around this time there was a secret meeting which took place in Kuwait between Zbigniew

Brezezinski, Saddam Hussein, the Kuwaiti Emir, and the Saudi rulers.

In this meeting, Brezezinski proposed to Saddam Hussein that he invade Iran and detach Khuzistan (oil producing province and Iran's primary source of income), thereby giving Iraq access to the Gulf through the Shatt-al-Arab, the narrow waterway between Iraq and Iran. Saddam Hussein was promised the financial support of the Kuwaiti and Saudi regimes for his invasion, an attack upon the Iranian revolution designed to prevent revolutionary sentiment from spreading among the oppressed peoples of the Emirates and of Saudi Arabia itself. When Saddam Hussein invaded Iran, Iraq had some $40 billion in hard currency reserves. The resistance of the Iranian population resulted in a protracted eight year war, during which Iraq was armed by the United Stated and Western Europe and bankrolled by the rulers of Kuwait and Saudi Arabia.

Iran-Contra Connection

While the U.S. was supplying arms to Iraq, it was also supplying arms to Iran with the intention of bleeding both countries dry. The fact that the U.S. supplied Iran with arms was made public during the Iran-Contra hearings. But what was not made public was that members of the Reagan-Bush campaign staff and representatives of the Iranian government met in Paris in October 1980, prior to the 1980 Presidential election. The attendees included George Bush, William Casey (former CIA director under Reagan), Richard Allen (former National Security Advisor under Reagan), and Donald Gregg (National Security Council staffer under Reagan, later Bush's aide, and now ambassador to South Korea). This group from the Reagan-Bush campaign was very concerned that the Carter administration would pull an "October Surprise" by negotiating the release of the U.S. Embassy hostages in Iran before the November election, which might have given Jimmy Carter enough momentum to win the election. In this meeting, the Iranians were promised that if they delayed the release of the hostages that the Reagan Administration would provide Iran with U.S. weapons and spare parts it needed in its war against Iraq. The hostages were released on January 20, 1981, the day of Ronald Reagan's inauguration as president.

In 1986, an Israeli government spokesman stated that Israel had been providing arms to Iran since 1982, and that the shipments had been made with the knowledge of the U.S. government. U.S. Representative Jim Wright (Dem., Texas) disclosed on November 20, 1986 that Israel, with the knowledge and approval of the U.S. government, had sent more than 2,000 anti-tank missiles and more than 200 Hawk anti-aircraft missiles, with the understanding that the U.S. government would replenish that material for the government of Israel.

North to the Rumaila Oil Reserve

Meanwhile, while Saddam Hussein was doing the bidding of the United States and Kuwaiti's ruler through the war against Iran, the Kuwaitis were steadily encroaching north, notably into the area overlapping the great Rumaila oil reserve of Iraq. Iraq's Foreign Minister, Tariq Aziz would observe:

> It should be noted that for the entire period... [when] Iraq was preoccupied with its internal problems and regional affairs, including most recently, the eight year long war between Iraq and Iran, the rulers of Kuwait were taking advantage of the situation to advance northwards, where they establish control posts, military installations, farms and oil facilities.

These encroachments were not haphazard. The floating border enlarged Kuwait by over 900 square miles until the southern tier of the Rumaila reserve was under Kuwaiti occupation.

The Sheikh then purchased the Santa Fe Drilling Corporation of Alhambra, California for a sum of $2.3 billion. Santa Fe Drilling was noted for its sophisticated "slant" drilling equipment, wherein oil drilling proceeded not vertically but horizontally. For years, Kuwait proceeded to drill deep into the Rumaila reserve in Iraq, extracting billions of dollars of Iraqi oil.

Santa Fe is a U.S.-based corporation that owns 275 oil and gas leases on 250,000 acres of U.S. government land. Its subsidiary, C.F. Braun, is a defense contractor developing U.S. nuclear weapons material. Persons who have served on the Board of Santa Fe include former President Gerald Ford, who named George Bush CIA Director, Brent Scowcroft, then an aide to Gerald Ford, who is now the National Security Advisor under George Bush. Also on the Board was Carla Hills' husband, Rodrick Hills. She is the Trade Representative in the Bush Administration and HUD Secretary under the Ford Administration.

Iraq's $80 Billion Debt

But the dispute between Iraq and Kuwait did not center solely on territory or physical possession of the oil reserves. Having fallen $80 billion in debt, Saddam Hussein was now pressed by Kuwait and Saudi Arabia for repayment with interest. The principle source of hard currency earnings, namely petroleum, was highly susceptible to price fluctuations pegged to production quotas.

Iraq and the other OPEC members began to argue for production quotas which would enable producing states to exercise some modicum of control over price structures. Although billions of dollars are earned from crude oil, these earnings pale before the profits made from refined products, and from the distribution and processing of petroleum.

With the end of the Iran-Iraq war, Saddam Hussein found that his former allies among the Emirates, Kuwait, Saudi Arabia and Egypt no longer were willing to hold to OPEC decisions on production. Even when decisions were taken to fix production levels, the Emirates, and notably Kuwait, would flood the market. Protests from Libya, Iran and others were met by increased naval activity in the Gulf by the United States.

In February 1990, Saddam Hussein spoke at the Amman Summit on the relationship between oil production and armed presence in the Gulf. Noting that the original pretext for the presence of the U.S. fleet, namely the Iran-Iraq war, was absent and yet the fleet remained and was being steadily augmented, Saddam Hussein began to sense that his usefulness to the United States was nearing an end. He said the following:

> The continued presence of the American fleet in the Gulf is due to the fact that, as a result of developments in the international political situation, developments in the prospects for the petroleum market and the growing need for petroleum among the Americans, Europeans, Japan, the East European States and the Soviet Union, the Gulf has emerged as the most important spot in the world...
>
> If the Gulf people and the rest of the Arabs along with them fail to take heed, the Arab Gulf region will be ruled by American will. Should weakness remain among us and we fail to heed what is now happening, matters will get to the point where the U.S. will dictate the quantity of oil or natural gas to be produced by each state, the quantity which can be sold to this or that state; and prices will be fixed - all on the basis of a special outlook which has to do solely with U.S. interests and in which no consideration is given to the interest of others.

Within days of this speech, the Western press began to carry stories about Saddam Hussein's missiles, chemical weapons, and nuclear potential. The Israeli press openly speculated about preemptive strikes on the model of the Israeli attack on Iraq's nuclear power plant in 1981. In addition, Tariq Aziz noted:

Immediately thereafter, the rulers of Kuwait - together with the Emirates - came up all of a sudden with calls for increases in their production quotas. Without waiting for discussion, they flooded the oil market with a huge surplus. Prices dropped from $21 per barrel to as little as $11 per barrel, which meant a loss of earnings amounting to billions of dollars under the trying circumstances for us brought about the huge cost of the war.

At the Arab Summit Conference in Baghdad from May 28-30, 1990, Saddam Hussein stated during a closed session:

War is at times waged by troops, and harm is inflicted by explosions, by slaughter and by coup attempts; at other times, it is inflicted by way of the economy. To those who have no intention of waging war against Iraq, I say this is a kind of war against us.

The Economic War Against Iraq

At the end of June, Iraqi Deputy Prime Minister, Saadoun Hammadi, carried personal appeals from Saddam Hussein to King Fahd of Saudi Arabia, Jaber al-Ahmad and Sheikh Zayed of the Emirates proposing a solution based upon standard production quotas - as has been set by OPEC on numerous earlier occasions. Iraq proposed that quotas should allow crude oil to market at $25 a barrel, a price which would permit reduction of the deficits arising from its war with Iran.

Being that price increases in crude oil bring billions in additional earnings to the producers, the insistent lowering of their own earnings could only be construed by Iraq as a political decision aimed at destabilizing the Iraqi economy and the regime itself. Iraq was rebuffed. Saddam Hussein now appealed for a meeting between the heads of state of Iraq, Kuwait, Saudi Arabia, and the Emirates. This request was refused. A meeting of the oil ministers was then proposed by Iraq.

The four oil ministers met on July 10, 1990. An agreement was reached to establish production quotas which would allow the price to float upward gradually. The day after the meeting had been concluded, however, the Kuwaiti oil minister announced to the press, after conferring with the Emir, that Kuwait would increase production substantially by October 1990.

On July 16, 1990, Saddam Hussein made a speech in which he asserted that the deliberate flooding of the market had caused the price of Iraqi oil to drop from $28 to $11 per barrel, a loss to the Iraqi economy of $14 billion in a matter of months. He accused the United States of orchestrating an economic war against Iraq and issued a warning that Iraq could not afford to accept passively an effort to undercut its economy:

> Iraqis, on whom this deliberate injustice has been inflicted, believe firmly in defending their rights and in self-defense. Better to be deprived of life than the means of living. If words fail to provide us with protection, then deeds are badly needed to restore rights to those whose rights have been usurped.

A final meeting was requested by Iraq, which occurred on July 30 in Jeddah, between Saddam Hussein and the Crown Prince of Kuwait. Kuwait would agree neither to production quotas nor to cease pumping oil from Iraq's Rumaila reserve. It would not forego any of Iraq's debt. Tariq Aziz concluded on September 4:

> It was inconceivable that a regime, such as that in Kuwait, could risk engaging in a conspiracy of such magnitude against a large, strong country such as Iraq, if it were not being supported and protected by a great power; and that power was the United States of America.

Deliberate Entrapment

On September 18, the Foreign Ministry of Iraq published verbatim the transcripts of meetings held between high ranking U.S. officials and Saddam Hussein just days before Iraqi troops entered Kuwait on August 2.

James McCartney, columnist for Knight-Ridder Newspaper's Washington Bureau, acknowledges that these transcripts are "not disputed by the State Department." On July 25, U.S. Ambassador April Glaspie, informed Saddam Hussein in her official capacity, "We have no opinion on...conflicts like your border disagreement with Kuwait."

Glaspie repeated this several times. To make sure the point was taken, she added, "Secretary of State James Baker has directed our official spokesman to emphasize this instruction." Indeed, Baker's official spokesperson, Margaret Tutwiler, and Assistant Secretary of State John Kelly, "both did exactly that. A week before the invasion both repeated publicly that the United States was not obligated to come to Kuwait's aid if it were attacked." (Santa Barbara News-Press, September 24, 1990).

McCartney is incredulous in reviewing the heavy-handedness with which the message was conveyed to Saddam Hussein. "At one point in the conversion, Glaspie said: 'I have direct instruction from the President...'"

Two days before Iraqi troops entered Kuwait, Assistant Secretary State John Kelly appeared before the House Foreign Affairs Sub-Committee, where Rep. Lee Hamilton (Dem., Ind.) asked him "if the United States was committed to come to Kuwait's defense." Later, Hamilton recalled Kelly before the Sub-Committee to remind him of their colloquy:

I asked you if there was a U.S. commitment to come to Kuwait's defense if it was attacked. Your response over and over again was: "We have no defense treaty relationship with any Gulf country."

McCartney, like Hamilton, concludes that the United States had, with deliberation, given Saddam Hussein "a green light for invasion. George Bush...left the door opened and Saddam Hussein walked through. And much blood may be [has been] shed as a result."

CHAPTER 6

THE TANGLED WEB

Oh, what a tangled web we weave
When first we practice to deceive

Sir Walter Scott

The Council on Foreign Relations and the Trilateral Commission, if you don't know about these organizations then I would highly recommend that you start learning. Here are some of the reasons why: Members of the power elite dominate the membership of these organizations; most of the U.S. Presidents and presidential candidates for the last 40 or so years were or are members of one or both of these organizations; most of Federal Reserve Board of Governors were or are members of one or both of these organizations; many U.S. Senators and Representatives were or are members of one or both of these organizations; most high-level federal government officials were or are members or one or both of these organizations; most of the people who are appointed to serve on presidential commissions were or are members of one or both of these organizations. In short these two organizations have a direct and substantial influence on the affairs of this nation and on your life.

Council on Foreign Relations

According to the literature, the Council on Foreign Relations (CFR) was founded in 1921 by bankers, lawyers, and academicians who were fully cognizant of the larger role the United States would play in world affairs as a result of World War I. The council has about 1,800 members, half from the New York area, half from the rest of the country. Before 1970 the members were primarily financiers, executives, and lawyers, with a strong minority of journalists, academic experts, and government officials. Since 1970 there has been an effort to include a larger number of government officials, including foreign-service officers, politicians, and staff members of congressional committees concerned with foreign policy.

The council receives its general funding from wealthy individuals, corporations, and subscriptions to its influential periodical, *Foreign Affairs*. For special projects, however, it often relies upon major foundations for support. In 1978-1979, for example, it received $66,000 from the Ford and Rockefeller foundations for its project on emerging issues in Africa, and in 1979-1980 its project on U.S.-Soviet relations received $55,000 from the Ford Foundation and $5,000 from the Mobil Oil Foundation.

The Council's discussion groups and projects very often lead the way for U.S. foreign policy initiatives. For example council groups called the War-Peace Study Groups met from 1940 to 1945 in order to develop plans for after World War II. They had a major influence in creating the International Monetary Fund, the World Bank, and the United Nations. A series of study groups in the 1940s and 1950s helped to establish the consensus wisdom that it was necessary to defend South Vietnam at all costs. Large foundation grants in the early 1960s led to study groups that reconsidered U.S. policy toward China, concluding that the policy must be changed to allow for recognition of its communist government and eventual trade relations.

We can get some idea of what goes in these discussion groups from the minutes of one of the Council's secret meetings entitled Intelligence and Foreign Policy held on January 8, 1968. The minutes were captured by anti-war protesters at Harvard University's Center for International Studies in 1971, and published by the Africa Research Group. The Discussion Leader of this meeting was Richard M. Bissell Jr., a former economics professor at Yale and MIT who joined the CIA in 1954. He was Deputy Director for Plans (head of clandestine services) from 1958 to 1962, but was fired by President John F. Kennedy after the Bay of Pigs fiasco. In this meeting the real purpose of the CIA, covert action, was discussed. Bissell described covert action as "attempting to influence the internal affairs of other nations--sometimes called 'intervention'-- by covert means. He went on to list the elements of covert action:

1. political advice and counsel;
2. subsidies to an individual;
3. financial support and "technical assistance" to political parties;
4. support of private organizations, including labor unions, business firms, cooperatives, etc.;
5. covert propaganda;
6. "private" training of individuals and exchange of persons;
7. economic operations;
8. paramilitary or political action operations designed to overthrow or to support a regime.

Trilateral Commission

In 1973 the Trilateral Commission was founded by David Rockefeller, Chase Manhattan Bank chairman, Zbigniew Brzezinski, Carter's national security advisor, and other like-minded "eminent private citizens." The Trilateral Commission consist of about 300 members from international business and banking, government, academia, media, and conservative labor. The Commission's purpose is to engineer an enduring partnership among the power elites of North America, Western Europe, and Japan - hence the term "trilateral" - in order to safeguard Western capitalism from challenges from underdeveloped countries.

An Abridged Who's Who

CFR - Council on Foreign Relations
TC - Trilateral Commission
Ch. - Chairman
Com. - Committee
Dir. - Director
Exec. - Executive
Gov. - Governor
Pres. - President
Sec. - Secretary

Tom Bradshaw - CFR; NBC.

Zbigniew Brzezinski - CFR. Dir.; TC, Dir.; National Security Advisor; Dir., Amnesty International; Dir., Foreign Affairs; Dir., Foreign Policy; Bilderberg; NAACP.

George Bush - CFR; TC; U.S. Pres., U.S. Vice-Pres.; Dir., CIA; Ch., Republican National Com.; Amb. to UN.

Jimmy Carter - TC; U.S. Pres.; Gov., Georgia; State Senator.

William T. Coleman, Jr. - CFR; TC, Exec. Com.; Senior Partner O'Melveny and Meyers; Ch. NAACP Legal Defense and Education Fund; Sec. of Transportation; Stock Exchange; Board of Dir.: IBM, Chase Manhattan Bank, Pespi Co., AMAX, American Can Co., Pan Am, Pennsylvania Mutual Life, Philadelphia Electric Co.

Alan Cranston - TC; U.S. Senate.

Thomas Foley - TC; Speaker, U.S. House of Rep.

Thomas Hughes - CFR; TC; Pres. Carnegie Endowment for International Peace; State Dept.

Charlene Hunter-Gault - CFR; PBS.

Lane Kirkland - CFR; TC; Pres. AFL-CIO; Co-Ch. Com. on Present Danger; Rockefeller Fund; African-American Labor Center; Carnegie Endowment for International Peace; Bilderberg.

Henry Kissinger - CFR; TC, Exec. Com.; Sec. of State; National Security Advisor; Ch., International Advisor Com. Chase Manhattan Bank, Bilderberg Steering Com.

Ted Koppel - CFR; ABC.

Walter Mondale - CFR; TC; U.S. Vice-Pres.; U.S. Senate, Bilderberg.

Dan Rather - CFR; CBS.

David Rockefeller - CFR, Ch.; TC, North American Ch.; Ch., Chase Manhattan Bank; Ch. Rockefeller Brother Fund; Bilderberg; Business Council; Business Roundtable.

Carl T. Rowan - TC; Columnist Chicago Daily News; Dir. U.S. Information Agency; Amb. to Finland.

Paul Volcker - CFR; TC; Ch. Federal Reserve Board; Chase Manhattan Bank; Treasury Dept.; Rockefeller Fund;

Casper Weinberger - CFR; TC; Sec. of Defense; Vice-Pres. and General Counsel Bechtel Corp.; Sec. of HEW; Board of Dir: Pespi Co., Quaker Oats Co.

Andrew Young - CFR; TC; Mayor, Atlanta; Amb. to UN; House of Rep.

Politics does indeed make strange bedfellows.

CHAPTER 7

GOVERNMENT FOR HIRE

> The public and leaders of most countries
> continue to live in a mental universe
> which no longer exist - a world of
> separate nations - and have great
> difficulties thinking in terms of global
> perspectives and interdependence.
> The liberal premise of a separation
> between the political and economic realm
> is obsolete: issues related to economics
> are the heart of modern politics.

> -Toward a Renovated International
> System
> (Trilateral Task Force Report: 1977)

Members of the international power elite are enable
to directly influence the federal government in ways
no other organizations can even come close to. Even
politicians with the best of intentions and the
strongest of wills find themselves virtually helpless
against the massive political influence and financial
backing of the power elites. The power elites are
enable to influence the federal government through
three basic processes:

1) The candidate-selection process, through which
   the members of the power elite attempt to
   influence electoral campaigns by means of

campaign finances and favors to political candidates.

2) The special-interest process, through which specific individuals, corporations, and industrial sectors realize their narrow and short-run interests on taxes, subsides, and regulation in dealing with congressional committees, regulatory bodies, and executive departments.

3) The policy-making process, through which the general policies of the policy-making network (which includes organizations like the Council on Foreign Relations) are brought to the White House and Congress.

The Candidate-Selection Process

The power elites involve themselves in the candidate-selection process through the simple, direct, often very unsubtle means of large campaign donations and other favors to political candidates that far outweigh what other classes and groups can muster. In the political system of the United States the fact that there are two major political parties is superfluous. The emphasis of elections in the U.S. is not the policies of the political parties or the candidates but the personal image and attributes of the individual candidates. This view is strongly supported by the statement of the executive director of a congressional watchdog organization, the National Committee for an effective Congress: "For all intents and purposes, the Democratic and Republican parties don't exist. There are only individuals (i.e., candidates) and professionals (i.e., consultants, pollsters, and media advisors)." It is because the candidate-selection process in the American political system is so individualistic, and therefore dependent upon name recognition and personal image, that it can be in good part dominated by members of the power elite through large campaign contributions. In the roles of both big donors and fund raisers, the power elites, the same people who control corporations and banks play a central role in the careers of most politicians who advance beyond the local level.

Financial Support to Candidates

There are numerous other methods besides campaign donations by which members of the corporate community can give financial support to politicians. One of the most direct is to give them stock or to purchase property from them at a price well beyond the market value. In 1956, to take one example, Texas millionaires wanted one of their corporate lawyers, Robert B. Anderson, to consider becoming the vice-presidential candidate on the Republican ticket. Anderson hesitated because he did not want to lower his income. To deal with this problem, several oilmen entered into a complex transaction in which Anderson purchased royalty interests for one dollar, then sold the leases a short time later at a profit of over $900,000 leaving him a millionaire and able to carry on his political career. In the event, he did not become the vice-presidential candidate but was appointed secretary of the treasury instead.

A somewhat similar case involved Ronald Reagan in 1966, just after he became governor of California. Twentieth Century-Fox purchased several hundred acres of his land adjacent to its large outdoor set in Malibu for nearly $2 million, triple its assessed market value and 30 times what he paid for it in 1952. The land was never utilized and was later sold to the state. It was this transaction, along with $20,000-an-appearance speeches to business and conservative groups, that gave Reagan the financial security that made it possible for him to devote full time to his political career.

In short, the campaign donations and the less obvious financial favors from members of the upper class and corporate community are a central element in determining who enters politics with any hope of winning a nomination. Campaign money is not the only element in the political process, as studies of high-spending losers reveal, but it is an very essential one given the need for name recognition. It is the need for a large amount of start-up money-- to travel around the district or the country, to send out large mailings, to schedule radio and television time in advance--that gives members of the power elite a very direct role in the process right from the start and thereby provides them with personal access to politicians of both parties.

Elected Officials in Top Income Bracket

What kinds of elected officials emerge from a political process that puts such great attention on campaign finance and media recognition? The answer is available from numerous studies. Politicians especially those who hold the highest elective offices, are first of all people from the top 10 to 15 percent of the occupational and income ladders. Only a minority are from the upper class or corporate community, but in a majority of cases they share in common a business and legal background with members of the upper class.

If we examine the background of U.S. presidents we will find that few twentieth-century Presidents have been from outside the very wealthiest circles. Theodore Roosevelt, William H. Taft, Franklin D. Roosevelt, and John F. Kennedy were from upper-class backgrounds. Herbert Hoover, Jimmy Carter, and Ronald Reagan were millionaires before they were deeply involved in national politics. Lyndon B. Johnson was a millionaire several times over through his wife's land dealing and his use of political leverage to gain a lucrative television license in Austin. Even Richard M. Nixon was a rich man when he finally attained the presidency in 1968, after earning high salaries as a corporate lawyer between 1963 and 1968 due to his ability to open political doors for corporate clients.

The Special-Interest Process

The special-interest process, as already noted, is the means by which specific individuals, corporations, or industries gain the favors, tax breaks, regulatory rulings, and other governmental supports they need to realize their short-run interests. It depends on the efforts of such people as lobbyists, lawyers who used to serve on congressional staffs or work in regulatory agencies, employees of trade associations, and corporate executives whose explicit function is governmental liaison.

The special-interest process is based upon a great amount of personal contact, which involves varying combinations of information, pressure, gifts, friendship, and--not least--implicit promises of lucrative private jobs in the future for those who might want them.

On the surface lobbying may appear to be a fragmented, disunited, and self-serving effort on the part of various corporations and organizations but in reality there is a definite method to this madness. The efforts of lobbyists must be taken into context with the policy-planning network to understand how theirs efforts come together.

The Policy-Making Process

The policy-making process is not as well known or studied as the special-interest process. It appears to be as detached from day-to-day events as the special-interest is completely immersed in them. It appears as concerned with fairness and the national interest as the special-interest process seems biased and self-seeking. "Nonpartisan" and "objective" are the catch words use to describe the organizations involve, and many of its members show a mild disdain for lobbyists. Compared with those who labor in the special-interest process, its members are much more likely to be from the wealthiest of families, the most prestigious of law schools and university institutes, and the highest levels of banks and corporations.

First, people from these organizations are regular members of the unpaid committees that advise specific departments of the executive branch on general policies. Second, they are prominent on the president commissions that have been appointed with regularity since World War II to make recommendations on a wide range of issues from foreign policy to highway construction. Third, they are members of two private organizations, the Business Council and the Business Roundtable, which are treated with the utmost respect and cordiality in Washington. Finally, they serve as informal advisors to the President in times of foreign-policy crisis, and they are appointed to government positions with a frequency far beyond what could be expected by chance.

The perspectives developed in the organizations of the policy-planning network (e.g., Council on Foreign Relations, Committee for Economic Development, Trilateral Commission, Committee on the Present Danger) reach government in a variety of ways. On the most general level, their reports, news releases, and interviews are read by elected officials and their staffs, if not in their original form, then as they summarized in the Washington Post, New York Times, and Wall Street Journal. Members of these organizations also testify before congressional committees and subcommittees that are writing legislation or preparing budget proposals. However, the most important involvements with government are more direct and formal in nature.

LAND OF THE FREE?

> In carrying out your government, why
> should you use killing at all? Let your
> evinced desires be for what is good,
> and the people will be good.
>
> Confucian

Is there really freedom of expression and freedom of
speech in the United States? Of course there is! As
long as you don't say certain things. For those
organizations that oppose U.S. policy, often their
members tend to say certain things.

The FBI's Crackdown on Political Dissension

In January 1988, the people of the United
States learned of a secret nationwide FBI campaign
against the domestic opponents of U.S. policy in
Central America. Government documents obtained
through the Freedom of Information Act show that
from 1981 through at least 1985, the FBI infiltrated
the Committee in Solidarity with the People of El
Salvador (CISPES) and disrupted its work all across
the country. The investigation eventually reached
into nearly every sector of the anti-intervention
movement, from the Maryknoll Sisters, the Southern
Christian Leadership Conference, and the New Jewish
Agenda to the United Auto Workers, the United Steel
Workers, U.S. Senator Christopher Dodd, and U.S.
Representatives Pat Schroeder and Jim Wright.
Some of the goals and the methods of this
campaign were revealed by a central participant,
Frank Varelli. Varelli admitted that from 1981

through 1984, the FBI paid him to infiltrate and "break" the Dallas, Texas chapter of CISPES. To this end, he and his cohorts put out bogus literature under the CISPES name, burglarized CISPES members' home, and paid right-wing students to start fights at CISPES rallies. Varelli was told to seduce an activist nun to get blackmail photos for the FBI. It was also suggested that he plant guns on CISPES members. As part of his work, he routinely exchanged information about U.S. and Central American activists with the Salvadoran National Guard, sponsor of that country's death squad.

In Albany, New York in 1981, the FBI and police infiltrated and disrupted the Capital District Coalition Against Apartheid and Racism (CDCAAR). At 3 a.m. on the day of the group's protest against the U.S. tour of the South African Springbok rugby team, FBI agents and the state and local police broke into the home of CDCAAR leader Vera Michelson. Supposedly acting on an anonymous FBI informer's false report that the anti-apartheid activists were stockpiling weapons, the officers burst into Michelson's bedroom, put a shotgun to her head, and forced her to crawl to another part of the apartment where she was handcuffed to a table. They then ransacked the apartment, confiscating CDCAAR files along with private papers and address books. Michelson and two other organizers were detained on bogus charges and kept from participating in the demonstration. They later learned that the same FBI infiltrator had spread false reports of planned violence in order to discourage participation in the demonstration.

Churches and organizations opposed to U.S. policy in Central America reported more than 300 incidents of harassment from 1984 through 1988, including nearly 100 break-ins. Important papers, files, and computer disks were stolen or found damaged and strewn about, while money and valuables were left untouched. License plates on a car seen fleeing an attempted burglary of the Washington D.C. office of Sojourners, a religious group that helped form the Pledge of Resistance to U.S. war in Central America, were trace to the U.S. National Security Agency. Other incidents were also attributed to government agents or to "private" right-wing groups backed by Lt. Col. Oliver North at the National Security Council. The FBI repeatedly rejected congressional calls for a federal probe.

Besides break-ins, excessive paramilitary might is often use against organizations that oppose U.S. policy. On October 18, 1984 eight New York City Black activists were arrested. A "Joint Anti-Terrorist Task Force" of more than 500 FBI and police agents, wielding machine guns and a bazooka, cordoned off entire city blocks to arrest law school graduates, city housing managers, college students, and a union steward. Promising community projects were disrupted while the eight were held for weeks without bail and placed for almost a year under strict curfew, while their co-workers were jailed for refusing to testify before a grand jury. Acquitted of the major charges when jurors rejected the claims of a police infiltrator, the eight faced continued police harassment. One was later framed on bogus weapon charges, along with two other leaders of a Brooklyn community group, Black Men Against Crack.

The FBI's Campaign Against Jesse Jackson

In Alabama, in the mid-1980s, the FBI mounted a massive effort to intimidate grassroots supporters of Jesse Jackson's presidential campaign and to crush the emerging pro-Jackson Black leadership based in the Campaign for a New South. Immediately after the September 1984 primaries in Alabama, as many as two hundred FBI agents swept through the five western Alabama Black Belt counties that had given their votes to Jesse Jackson, rousing elderly people from their beds in the middle of the night, taking about one thousand of them in police-escorted buses to Mobile to be finger-printed, and suggested that their absentee ballots may have been tampered with by the civil rights workers who had secured their votes. The offices of civil rights worker were also raided and some of the documents they needed for the November elections were confiscated.

In January 1985, indictments for vote and mail fraud were handed down against eight of the Black Belt's most experienced organizers and political leaders. In bringing the indictments, the federal government used the Voting Rights Act of 1965, the very act most of these people had marched from Selma to Montgomery to get enacted. Although the defendants were acquitted of all major charges and their organizations survived, the raids, interrogation, arrests, and trails took a heavy toll.

COINTELPRO

Government harassment of U.S. political activists clearly exists today, violating our fundamental constitutional rights and creating a climate of fear and distrust which undermines any effort to challenge official policy. Similar attacks on social justice movements came to light during the 1960s. Only years later did we learn that these were just the tip of the iceberg. Largely hidden at the time was a vast government program to neutralize domestic political opposition through "covert action" (political repression carried out secretly or under the guise of legitimate law enforcement). The FBI used its Counterintelligence Program (COINTELPRO) to carry out these "covert actions."

When congressional investigations, political trials, and other traditional legal modes of repression failed to counter growing movements, and even helped to fuel them, the FBI and police moved outside the law. They resorted to the secret and systematic use of fraud and force to sabotage constitutionally protected political activity. Their methods ranged far beyond surveillance, amounting to homefront version of the convert action for which the CIA has become infamous throughout the world.

FBI Headquarters secretly instructed [refer to Appendix B] its field offices to propose schemes to "expose, disrupt, misdirect, discredit, or otherwise neutralize" specific individuals and groups. Close coordination with local police and prosecutors was strongly encouraged. Other recommended collaborators included friendly news media, business and foundation executives, and university, church, and trade union officials, as well as such "patriotic" organizations as the American Legion.

Final authority rested with FBI Headquarters in Washington, D.C. Top FBI officials pressed local field offices to step up their activity and demanded regular progress reports. Agents were directed to maintain full secrecy "such that under no circumstances should the existence of the program be made known outside the Bureau and appropriate within-office security should be afforded to sensitive operations and techniques. A total of 2,370 officially approved COINTELPRO actions were admitted to the Senate Intelligence Committee, and thousands more have since been uncovered.

The FBI's Campaign Against Black Nationalists

COINTELPRO operations were supposedly terminated in the early 1970s but the FBI and other law enforcement officials continue their attack on organizations, they especially targeted Black Nationalist or self-help organizations. In Mississippi, federal and state agents attempted to discredit and disrupt the United League of Marshall County, a broad-based grassroots civil rights group struggling to stop Klan violence. In California, a notorious paid operative for the FBI, Darthard Perry, code-named "Othello," infiltrated and disrupted local Black groups and took personal credit for the fire that razed the Watts Writers Workshop's multi-million dollar cultural center in Los Angles in 1973. The Los Angles Police Department later admitted infiltrating at least seven 1970s community groups, including the Black-led Coalition Against Police Abuse.

In the mid-1970s, the U.S. Bureau of Alcohol, Tobacco and Firearms (ATF) conspired with the

Wilmington, North Carolina police to frame nine local civil rights workers and the Rev. Ben Chavis, field organizer for the Commission for Racial Justice of the United Church of Christ. Chavis had been sent to North Carolina to help Black communities respond to escalating racist violence against school desegregation. Instead of arresting Klansmen, the ATF and police coerced three young Black prisoners into falsely accusing Chavis and the others of burning white-owned property. Although all three prisoners later admitted they had lied in response to official threats and brides, the FBI found no impropriety. The courts repeatedly refused to reopen the case and the Wilmington Ten served many years in prison before pressure from international religious and human rights groups won their release.

As the Republic of New Afrika (RNA) began to build autonomous Black economic and political institutions in the deep South, the Bureau repeatedly disrupted its meetings and blocked its attempts to buy land. On August 18, 1971, the FBI and police launched an armed pre-dawn assault on national RNA offices in Jackson, Mississippi. Carrying a warrant for a fugitive who had been brought to RNA Headquarters by FBI informer Thomas Spells, the attackers concentrated their fire where the informer's floor plan indicated the RNA President Imari Obadele slept. Though Obadele was away at the time of the raid, the Bureau had him arrested and imprisoned on charges of conspiracy to assault a government agent.

The COINTELPRO-triggered collapse of the Black Panthers' organization and their supporters in the winter of 1971 left them defenseless as the government moved to prevent them from regrouping. On August 21, 1971, national Party officer George Jackson, world-renowned author of the political autobiography *Soledad Brother*, was murdered by San Quentin prison authorities on the pretext of an attempted jailbreak. In July 1972, southern California Panther leader Elmer "Geronimo" Pratt was successful framed for a senseless $70 robbery-murder committed while he was hundreds of miles away in Oakland, California, attending Black Panther meetings for which the FBI managed to "lose" all of its surveillance records. Documents obtained through the Freedom of Information Act later revealed that at least two FBI agents had infiltrated Pratt's defense committee. They also indicated that the state's main witness, Julio Butler, was a paid informer who had worked in the Party under the direction of the FBI and the Los Angles Police Department. For many years, FBI Director Webster publicly denied that Pratt had ever been a COINTELPRO target, despite the documentary proof in his own agency's records.

Also targeted well into the 1970s were former Panthers assigned to form underground to defend against armed government attack on the Party. It was they who had regrouped as the Black Liberation Army (BLA) when the Party was destroyed. FBI files show that, within a month of the close of COINTELPRO, further Bureau operations against the BLA were mapped out in secret meetings convened by presidential aide John Ehrlichman and attended by President Nixon and Attorney General Mitchell. In the following years, many former Panther leaders were murdered by the police in supposed "shoot-outs" with the BLA. Others such as Sundiata Acoli, Assata Shakur, Dhoruba Al-Mujahid Bin Wahad (formerly Richard Moore), and the New York 3 (Herman Bell, Anthony "Jalil" Bottom, and Albert "Nuh" Washington) were sentenced to long prison terms after rigged trials.

In the case of the New York 3, FBI ballistics reports withheld during their mid-1970s trial show that bullets from an alleged murder weapon did not match those found at the site of the killings for which they are still serving life terms. The star witness against them has publicly recanted his testimony, swearing that he lied after being tortured by the police (who repeatedly jammed an electrical cattleprod into his testicle) and secretly threatened by the prosecutor and judge. The same judge later dismissed petitions to reopen the case, refusing to hold any hearing or to disqualify himself, even though his misconduct is a major issue. As the NY3 continued to press for a new trial, their evidence was ignored by the news media while the former prosecutor's one-sided, racist "docudrama" on the case, Badge of the Assassin, aired on national television.

Political Assassinations

While activists from all walks of life were randomly beaten and killed by police and guardsmen, Black leaders targeted under COINTELPRO faced "neutralization" through premeditated murder. In Houston, Texas, in July 1970, police assassinated Carl Hampton, Black leader of that city's burgeoning Peoples Party. In Oakland, California, in April 1968, Bobby Hutton, national finance minister of the Black Panther Party, was gunned down as he emerged unarmed, hands held high from the police ambush which drove Eldridge Cleaver into exile. In Chicago, in December 1969, the FBI, police, and state's attorney joined forces in the cold-blooded murder of Illinois Black Panther Party chairman Fred Hampton.

The murder of Fred Hampton was especially pivotal. Hampton was a charismatic leader who developed a broad following in the Black community and organized the first multi-racial "rainbow coalition." In the late fall of 1969, he agreed to take the reins of the national party organization after its initial leaders were jailed or forced into exile. At that point, having failed in its efforts to get Hampton rubbed out by local street gangs, the FBI arranged to have the job done by a special squad of police assigned to the state's attorney office.

The Bureau provided a detailed floorplan of Hampton's home marked to show where Hampton slept. Its paid informer, William O'Neal, Hampton's personal bodyguard, drugged Hampton's Kool-Aid so he would remain unconscious through the night. As the Panthers slept, O'Neal slipped out and a 14-man hit squad armed with automatic weapons crashed into Hampton's home and pumped in over 200 rounds of ammunition. When their fire subsided, Hampton and Mark Clark lay dead and seven other Panthers were wounded.

The incident was subsequently investigated by a blue-ribbon citizens' commission and litigated at length in the federal courts. Despite an elaborate law enforcement cover-up, Hampton's death was found to be the not of a shootout, as claimed by the authorities, but of a carefully orchestrated, Vietnam-style "search and destroy" mission. The federal and local governments had to pay $1.8 million in damages to the parents and survivors.

CHAPTER 8

JUST SAY NO?

> Ye shall know the truth and the truth
> shall make you free.
>
> Motto of the CIA

Often when a person or a government becomes an enemy of the United State that person or government is accused of drug trafficking. The media hype concerning the "Drug Crisis" in this country is so great and so hypocritical that the general public is trained to automatically view anyone or anything mentioned with drugs in the same sentence as "evil" and "corrupt."

In 1986 the hype over the "Drug Crisis" was at its peak. The Hegelian methods used helped the Reagan Administration attack domestic freedoms and divert attention from more pressing social problems. These attacks were especially vicious and crude to Blacks.

Don't Believe the Hype

Throughout 1986, articles and TV news reports on illegal drugs, especially crack, flooded the media. From March to October 1986, NBC news aired more than 400 reports on drugs. CBS received the highest rating ever recorded for a documentary with its "48 Hours on Crack Street." And along with hundreds of other articles, the New York Times ran almost two

81

full pages daily for the week of the President and First Lady's drug crisis living speech.

The reality on the matter was that there was no "Drug Crisis." The use of illegal drugs - with the exception of crack - continued a years-long decline. While *Newsweek* editorialized that "an epidemic is abroad in America, as pervasive and dangerous in its way as the plagues of medieval times," the actual number of drug users in the U.S. decreased, especially among the young.

The absence of an epidemic is confirmed by figures from the National Institute on Drug Abuse (NIDA), the primary governmental body charged with monitoring drug usage. NIDA statistics show that the number of hospital emergency room admissions and deaths associated with drugs stayed fairly constant from 1983 though 1986. At the height of the "crisis" the numbers dying from cocaine still did not greatly exceed the total dying from over-the-counter painkillers like aspirin. Alcohol in combination with other drugs killed twice as many as cocaine.

The Sandinistas and Drug Trafficking

The disinformation campaign against the Sandinista government in Nicaragua is a prime example of how the U.S. government tries to influence public opinion to promote one of its policies. The first accusations of Sandinista drug running were reported in the Washington Times, on July 17, 1984. In the Times, which has ties to Reverend Sun Myung Moon's Unification Church, there was a story that linked "important members of the Marxist government in Nicaragua" with drug trafficking. The paper based this report on unnamed sources in the Reagan administration who referred to the statements of Federico Vaughan, a convicted drug dealer who worked as an informant for the U.S. government. They claimed that Vaughan, while testifying in a Miami court, hinted that members of the Nicaraguan government were involve in drug smuggling from Colombia to U.S., via Nicaragua.

Relying on the same unnamed sources, the New York Times, Los Angles Times and NBC-TV started to play up stories of the alleged connection between Nicaragua and "narco-terrorism." Then in October 1984, the *New York Times*, the *Wall Street Journal* and CBS-TV news reported that fugitive banker Robert Vesco was helping to finance cocaine trafficking by the Nicaraguan government. Citing "U.S. Customs sources," the reports said that Vesco had worked together with Federico Vaughan.

However, the federal judge in Miami, who heard Vaughan's case, found no traces of the alleged connection between Vaughan and Vesco, nor did he find any proof of relations between Vaughan and the Sandinista leadership. A study done by the *Columbia Journalism Review* noted that the judge's findings were never mentioned in major newspapers or on the major network news broadcasts.

The attack by the Reagan administration continued, however. On March 16, 1986, three months before Congress approved $100 million in aid for the contras, Reagan declared on national TV: "I know that all American parents who are concerned about the drug problem will be enraged to hear that high-ranking members of the Nicaraguan government are deeply involved in drug trafficking."

The U.S. Government and Drug Trafficking

The truth of the matter is that the evidence shows that the American government and not the Nicaraguan government was facilitating the importation of cocaine into the United States. The evidence shows that the CIA tapped into the South American-U.S. drug trade to keep the Nicaraguan contras armed and fighting during the two-year prohibition against U.S. support.

The evidence from king pin traffickers, contras, U.S. mercenaries, and congressional investigators strongly suggests extensive CIA involvement in the cocaine trade, from a top cocaine producing family in South America to the pilots who transport drugs.

Blaming the contras for drug trafficking, as few in the press and Congress have done, misses the point - the contras are a CIA operation. Yet, it would also be mistaken to isolate the CIA as the culprit from the larger White House conspiracy, managed by Lt. Col. Oliver North. Reagan's contra pipeline - as laid out in the joint House-Senate hearings - apparently utilized well-known drug traffickers in Miami and Costa Rica to fund and organize weapons shipments.

Nothing better indicates the depth of U.S. government involvement in drug trafficking than its direct dealings with the family of Jorge Ochoa, one of Colombia's two largest drug exporters, according to one account. The Agency apparently obtained cocaine directly from the Ochoa in Colombia. To move the illicit substance, the CIA also recruited drug traffickers who piloted the narcotics from Colombia north to refueling points in the northern Costa Rican jungle.

Costa Rica was the location where CIA-backed smugglers interfaced with the contra military operation. For the traffickers, Costa Rica's geographical location between Colombia and the United States made it a perfect transshipment point. A CIA operative, John Hull, allowed the traffickers to use several small jungle airstrips under his control to refuel and store cocaine before shipping it to the United States. In return, they paid user fees and made payoffs to the contras, and on return trips from southern Florida, the traffickers brought plane loads of weapons.

The Cover-up

Evidence that the CIA has actively tried to cover up its involvement in drug trafficking comes from a transcript of June 1986, Senate Foreign Relations Committee meeting. The CIA apparently blocked federal drug investigations of contra supporters to prevent the evidence from spreading. At the meeting, Senator John Kerry said:

I am incensed at the notion that in the name of...national security we are allowing drugs to come into this country....

The contra infrastructure consists of supply lines for the contras, used to move men, money, and supplies and, munitions to the contras.... They have been able to gain a license, if you will, of access to airfields, of the muting of Customs officials, an ability to be able to circumvent the law, in the name of national security. And in the name of national security, we can produce specific law enforcement officials who will tell you that they have been called off drug trafficking investigations because the CIA is involved or because it would threaten national security.

One federal drug investigation that was called off targeted FDN leader Enrique Bermudez. About Bermudez, Kerry said:

He was the target of a government-sponsored sting operation. He has been involved in drug running.... And the law enforcement officials know that the sting operation was called back in the interest of protecting the contras.

When asked by Senator Nancy Kassenbaum (Rep. Kans.) about approaching the CIA for help with the Senate investigation, Kerry said:

Let me say that I would be amazed if the CIA were to be very cooperative in this. We had a meeting with the CIA. [They] jumped out of their seats at some of the stuff that they heard we were thinking of looking at.

The cover up has also been helped along by the appointment of a 35-year CIA veteran to the House-Senate investigation to probe CIA wrongdoing in Costa Rica. Thomas Polgar, a former CIA station chief in Vietnam, is also currently an active member of the Virginia-based Association of Former

Intelligence Officers, a CIA lobbying organization. Polgar traveled to Costa Rica in April 1987, was led around by the U.S. embassy there which was deeply involved in the arms network, and didn't bother to interview Hull and others linked to CIA trafficking in Costa Rica. Polgar did, however, reveal what side of the investigation he was on when he told local reporters at the *Tico Times*, a Costa Rican weekly, that he doubted that "a conservative farmer like Hull would traffic in drugs."

The U.S. and Drugs: A Little History

U.S. government involvement in international drug trafficking is not a recent phenomena it goes back at least to the turn of the 20th century. In 1900, over 19,000 British, American, Russian, Japanese, and French soldiers crushed the Boxer Rebellion to ensure that China would keep it ports open to foreign trade (including opium). The Boxers, officially known as I Ho Ch'uan (The Righteous and Harmonious Fists), were oppose to foreign influence that to them was destroying China and Chinese culture. The Boxers rebelled because many of the injustices which caused the Opium Wars (1839-42, 1856-60) were still unresolved. In the Opium Wars the Chinese attempted to bar illegal importation of opium by British and French merchants.

In more recent history in Asia, after World War II, the CIA-backed Kuomintang (KMT or Chinese Nationalist Party) troops settled in Burma and controlled the opium traffic for buyers in northern Thailand and Bangkok. From 1948 on, American intelligence activities in the Golden Triangle were intertwined with the opium trade. Infiltration routes for CIA commando teams into southern China were also used as drug smuggling routes for traffickers in Burma and Thailand. Local Shan tribesmen provided the guides to both the Agency's teams and opium caravans near the Burma-Chinese border. And the Agency had maintained five secret training camps and two key listening posts in the Shan states protected by its drug smuggling KMT troops and local tribesmen.

During this time as is the case today, Thailand had become a major opium marketplace at the tip of the Golden Triangle. The military cliques of strongmen which ruled the country, beginning with General Phao Siyanon in 1947, also controlled the Thai National Police Department (TNPD) which was the largest opium traffic syndicate in the country. These "strongmen" grew immensely wealthy from their drug monopoly and from ties to the CIA. Much of this drug smuggling network remains very active today, and has deep roots in Thailand's military and paramilitary circles.

The CIA's role in Southeast Asia was a very pervasive one. The CIA founded and trained General Phao's paramilitary police force, and equipped it with artillery, tanks, and helicopters. The police force not only protected Thai borders but also conducted commando missions into Indochina, Burma, and China. U.S. paramilitary specialists, either retired military personnel or detailed personnel from other departments, were brought to Bangkok to train the new Border Patrol Police (BPP).

To manage the training and equipping of the BPP, the CIA had asked a retired OSS (predecessor to the CIA) China hand, the late Paul Helliwell, to form a cover organization out of Miami, the Overseas Southeast Asia Supply Company, or Sea Supply. Sea Supply had the sole contract with Thailand for services to the BPP. Helliwell also Thailand's Consul in Miami during the early 1950s, was one of the CIA's specialists on forming front companies and laundering funds for "black" operations in the Caribbean in support of the Agency's secret war against Cuba, especially in preparation for the 1961 Bay of Pigs invasion. The Agency's primary airline, Civil Air Transport (CAT), renamed Air America in the late 1960s, flew military equipment from CIA depots in Okinawa to Bangkok for Sea Supply. Within the Thailand-Burma theater, CAT flights carried weapons, paramilitary personnel, and opium for the Thai strongmen as well.

These operations continued and in the late 1960s several key players in the weapon supply network to the contras developed their skills in drug trafficking and secret war management in Southeast Asia. Theodore Shackley was CIA station chief in Laos from 1966 to 1969 and the de facto chief of staff for the Agency's secret war. Shackley later did a tour in South Vietnam where he managed Operation Phoenix, the "pacification" program against the Vietnamese. Tom Clines (convicted on September 18, 1990 of four income tax charges arising from his part in the Iran-Contra related "Enterprise" of General Richard Secord) worked under him in Laos, managing ground support activities for the war. Richard Secord, then a lieutenant colonel detailed to the Agency, was handling air support which included Air America and other minor CIA proprietary airlines. Secord stayed on in Thailand in the early 1970s to manage operations by U.S. Special Forces and Hmong (the Meo people of Southeast Asia who supported the U.S. in the Vietnam War) troops in Laos.

Together with Robert "Red" Jantzen, the Agency's station chief in Thailand (1958-1969) and Edwin Wilson, Shackley, Clines and Secord were cited in the late 1970s in the scandal of the collapse of the Nugan Hand Bank in Australia. The bank was found to be heavily involved in drug trafficking between Thailand and Australia, as well as money laundering and weapons deals in southern Africa and Asia.

CHAPTER 10

THE WONDERS OF SCIENCE

Cured yesterday of the disease,
I died last night of my physician

Matthew Prior

U.S. history is chock-full with efforts to inflict disease and death on so-called Third World people, both inside and outside U.S. borders, through chemical and biological warfare (CBW), medical experiments, and population control. Despite an alleged "ban" on development of CBW weapons since 1969, there is ample evidence that such programs have continued.

Chemical warfare is the use of chemicals to kill, incapacitate, or harm humans, animals, or plants; biological warfare is the use of disease-causing germs to do the same thing. CBW is simply a further extension of other military, economical, and political measures directed against the peoples of "enemy" nation.

CBW: Some History

The first recorded instance of U.S. biological warfare was in 1763, when colonial settlers gave smallpox-infested blankets to Native Americans who sought friendly relations. Many died as a result.

This tactic was repeated during the "Trail of Tears" of the 1800s.

In the Korean War (1950-53), according to an international investigating commission, the U.S. used an array of germ weapons against North Korea: feathers infected with anthrax; lice, fleas, and mosquitoes dosed with plague and yellow fever; diseased rodents; and various implements contaminated with deadly microbes--toilet paper, envelopes and the ink in fountain pens. In 1958, the Eisenhower administration pressed sedition charges against the three who had published these germ warfare charges in *China Monthly Review*, John Powell, Sylvia Powell, and Julian Schuman, but failed to get convictions.

In the Vietnam War, U.S. CBW reached its zenith. It was the most massive chemical war in history. Seeking to destroy crops supporting the popular guerrilla movements, the U.S. aerially sprayed 55 million kilograms (121 million pounds) of defoliants, primary Agent Orange, on the nations of Southeast Asia. As a result, the ecology of massive areas was destroyed, millions of people were poisoned, many developed cancer, some died, and the next generation suffered an extremely high rate of birth defects. Among the victims were many U.S. troops present in sprayed areas. In addition, CS gas, an anti-personnel gas, was massively used to force people out of enclosed areas. It often directly killed or maimed its targets.

Since its 1959 revolution, Cuba has been a prime target of U.S. military, economic, and political attacks. In the 1960s, an "anti-crop warfare" program was carried out. In 1971, the CIA infected Cuban pigs with African Swine Fever, a deadly disease; Cuban authorities had to slaughter the entire pig population to stop the disease's spread. A second such epidemic occurred in 1980, with equally devastating consequences, it was of unknown but suspicious origins. That was the same year that the blue mold decimated the tobacco harvest and a damaging rust disease hit the sugar cane crop. The Nation called this "a conjunction of plagues that would lead people less paranoid about the U.S. than the Cubans to wonder whether human hands had played a role in these natural disasters." The next year, an epidemic of dengue hemorrhagic fever--a painful mosquito-borne disease involving bone-breaking pain, flu symptoms, internal bleeding and shock--struck 300,000 Cubans and claimed 158 lives (including 101 children). An investigation done by *Covert Action Information Bulletin* produced strong evidence that the CIA released dengue-infected mosquitoes on the island. Court testimony in 1984 by a Cuban counterrevolutionary terrorist also supports this conclusion.

CBW: Use on Black People

From 1956 to 1958, in the poor Black communities of Savannah, Georgia, and Avon Park, Florida, the Army carried out field test with mosquitoes that may have been infected with yellow fever. The insects were released into residential areas from ground level and dropped from planes and helicopters. Many people were swarmed by mosquitoes and then developed unknown fevers; some died. After each test, Army agents posing as public health officials photographed and tested victims and then disappeared from town.

One highly suspicious incident that could bear scrutiny as a possible CBW test is the 1978 "mass suicide" of 900 people, most of whom were Black, in Jonestown, Guyana. John Judge, a Philadelphia activist who has extensively investigated the incident, notes that many of the drugs found there were the same ones tested under MKULTRA (CIA mind control experiments). The Guyanese Chief Medical Examiner testified in court that 80 percent of the bodies he examined showed signs of forcible injections. Jim Jones, the self-proclaimed leader of the "People's Temple" which moved to Guyana from San Francisco, and one of his aides, had CIA connections. The father of Jonestown leader Larry Layton was head of CBW Research at the Army's

Dugway Proving Grounds in the 1950s. The elder Layton admitted contributing $25,000 to the People's Temple. According to Judge, "Public exposure [in the mid-1970s] of experiments in U.S. prisons and mental institutions was, in all likelihood, a major impetus for relocating this testing to the jungle of a virtually unknown country.

From 1965 to 1968, 70 prisoners, mostly Black, at Holmesburg State Prison in Philadelphia, were the subjects of tests by Dow Chemical Company on the effects of dioxin, the highly toxic chemical contaminant in Agent Orange. Their skins were deliberately exposed to large doses and then monitored to watch the results. According to the doctor in charge, Albert Kligman, a University of Pennsylvania dermatologist, several subjects developed lesions which "lasted for four to seven months, since no effort was made to speed healing by active treatment." At a 1980 federal Environmental Protection Agency hearing where the experiment came to light, Kligman testified that no follow-up was done on the subjects for possible development of cancer. This was the second such experiment commissioned by Dow, the previous one carried out on 51 "volunteers," believed also to have been prisoners.

The Tuskegee Syphilis Experiment

In 1932, the U.S. Public Health Service initiated a study of untreated tertiary (third stage) syphilis using poor, uneducated Black men in Tuskegee, Alabama. Four hundred syphilitics were never told of their illness and were denied treatment. Another 200 healthy Black men were used as control subjects. Both groups were carefully monitored. According to the authoritative book on the subject, *Bad Blood*, by James H. Jones, "as of 1969, at least 28 and perhaps as many as 100 men had died as a direct result of complications caused by syphilis. Others had developed syphilis-related heart conditions that may have contributed to their deaths. Many wives of the untreated men may also have been infected; some children may have been born with congenital defects.

The experiments continued until 1972, when a outraged federal worker blew the whistle to the press, and nationwide condemnation forced the government to cancel the project. This employee had protested privately as far back as 1966, only provoking increasingly high-level secret meetings which resolved to continue the project. In 1972, as they reluctantly ordered its end, federal health officials hypocritically joined the press denunciations while implicitly defending the study as legitimate in its time. The survivors still received no treatment until eight months later, on the eve of congressional hearings. The federal office supervising the study was the predecessor of today's Centers for Disease Control (CDC) unit in charge of the AIDS program. The CDC, a journalist wrote in 1972, "sees the poor, the black, the illiterate and the defenseless in American society as a vast experimental resource for the government."

Concerning the connection between the CDC and AIDS, one should also note that Dr. David Sencer, the Director of the CDC who approved the continuation of the Tuskegee study in 1969, became New York City Health Commissioner, and a key player in AIDS policy, in the early 1980s. Concerning the connection between tertiary syphilis and AIDS, one should note that in February 1987, a New York doctor announced test results showing that all of his AIDS patients had previously undiagnosed (and thus untreated) cases of tertiary syphilis, and proposed that this may turn out to be the cause of AIDS .

CHAPTER 11

A GERM TOO FAR

> The diagnosis of disease is often easy,
> often difficult, and often impossible.
>
> Peter Mere Latham

AIDS, acquired immune deficiency syndrome, may be the most peculiar, as well as the most publicized, epidemic in human history. Yet it is quite possible that contrary to the conventional wisdom that AIDS has non-viral causes and transmission of the disease may not be from one victim to another exclusively.

Dr. Gallo and HIV

In 1981, Dr. Robert C. Gallo, the head of the Laboratory of Tumor Cell Biology at the National Cancer Institute in Bethesda, Maryland, assembled a team to spearhead AIDS research, and in 1984 he identified HTLV-III (human T-lymphotropic virus III) as the causal virus. In a 1987 article in Scientific American he stated categorically that the cause of AIDS "was conclusively shown to be the third human retrovirus," HTLV-III (later renamed HIV). This is the view to which most Americans have become persuaded: that the cause, and the only cause, of AIDS is this particular virus alone, transmitted from one victim to another.

Interest in AIDS is particularly intense in New York, with more definitely identified cases than anywhere else in the world. A $5.2 million AIDS Institute was established in 1983 within the State Health Department. In September 1985, in publications directed both to the general public and to the gay community, that Institute stated that:

...no one knows for sure what causes AIDS. Antibodies to a recently discovered virus have been found in the blood of most AIDS patients. It is not known whether this virus is the direct cause of AIDS, or is a result of having a damaged immune system.

On September 27, 1985, Science magazine published a comprehensive review of "The Epidemiology of AIDS: Current Status and Future Prospects," prepared by the federal Centers for Disease Control in Atlanta, Georgia, in which the role or non-viral agents in causing the disease--even as co-factors--was very much downplayed. The idea that the disease is caused only by the virus, and spread only from victim to victim, received another authoritative presentation in December 1986 and January 1987 issues of Scientific American, in articles by Dr. Gallo, considered the outstanding exponent of the view that HIV is the cause of AIDS and credited with discovering "the link between retroviruses and human leukemia and lymphoma."

But even before Dr. Gallo's much-ballyhooed "discovery" of HIV, and certainly since, published questions have appeared about AIDS in general and HIV in particular. Those who have dared to question the accepted dogma have been ridiculed, attacked, and most often, ignored by the medical establishment--in particular the Centers for Disease Control, the National Institutes of Health, and the American Medical Association.

The Evidence Against HIV

Dr. Joseph Sonnabend, a New York City physician who co-founded the AIDS Medical Foundation (later renamed the American Foundation for AIDS Research), has argued since 1983 that among gay men, "multiple factors, rather than a novel virus, probably induce AIDS," citing such factors as recurrent cytomegalovirus (CMV) infection and the immune suppression caused by repeated rectal deposits of semen. In 1983, Dr. Sonnabend founded and became editor of a professional journal called AIDS Research, which was open to all points of view on HIV. In December 1986, after ten issues, the publisher was persuaded by Max Essex, a Harvard scientist and close associate of Dr. Gallo, to fire Dr. Sonnabend and nearly all the editorial board. The journal's name was changed to AIDS Research and Human Retroviruses, and the new editorial board, which includes Dr. Gallo, is dominated by government, military, and corporate scientists.

The most authoritative critique of the HIV theory to date is by Professor Peter H. Duesberg of the University of California at Berkeley, who discussed the role of retroviruses in causing disease in a review article in March 1, 1987 Cancer Research. Disagreeing with Dr. Gallo, he questioned the role retroviruses are said to play in causing leukemia and lymphoma. He also stated categorically that:

> the AIDS virus is not sufficient to cause AIDS and that there is no evidence, besides its presence in a latent form, that it is necessary for AIDS.... the only support for the hypothesis that the AIDS virus causes AIDS is that 90% of the AIDS patients have antibody to the to the virus.

He also notes that the presence of antibodies appears to be of no significance to non-members of "risk groups," although he does say that the virus may "be directly responsible for early, mononucleosis-like disease observed in several infections prior to antiviral immunity." He also explains that since nearly everyone with the virus also has antibodies, "vaccination is not likely to benefit virus carriers with or without AIDS." This belies the feverish push by the CDC and other medical researchers for a vaccine against HIV which would supposedly prevent AIDS."

But if HIV does not produce the immune deficiency which characterizes AIDS, what does? Chemicals certainly might; why are they not being looked into? And why, with all the research data available that supports causes of AIDS other than HIV, has
the American media virtually ignored it?

Other Causes of Immune Deficiency

We have long known that immune systems can be harmed in many ways, including damage caused by toxic chemicals, by radiation, and by other factors. All three of the diseases for which retroviruses are blamed--leukemia, lymphoma, and immune deficiency syndromes--can also be caused by chemicals, including radioactive substances. Indeed the greatest leukemia epidemic in history was produced by the radioactivity following the atomic bombing of Japan. Few people realize that other consequences of the bombing were increased incidences of both lymphoma and immune deficiency. Other new and peculiar diseases from which Americans now suffer include toxic shock syndrome, Legionnaires' disease, Epstein-Barr syndrome, and swine flu vaccine reactions. When epidemic diseases can be produced by several different causes, all such possibilities require investigation.

Radioactive Waste

In light of the radioactive waste created by the legacy of the arms race, radioactive contamination should not be discounted when considering disease in the United States. In the August 1988 issue of Technology Review, Robert Alvarez and Arjun Makhijani described the extent of the problem in their article "Radioactive Waste: Hidden Legacy of the Arms Race":

> Billions of gallons of radioactive wastes from making bomb-grade material have been dumped directly into the soil and the groundwater. Millions more gallons of concentrated waste have been stored in tanks, many of which have leaked. These wastes are now beginning to contaminate public water supplies. The wastes also form explosive gases that could rip the tanks open and spew the material over a large area, creating a Chernobyl-scale accident.

At one site, Hanford, in Washington, the Department of Energy (DOE) has allowed 200 billion gallons of radioactive waste to be dumped directly into the soil through shallow evaporation ponds, seepage basins, and burial pits--enough waste to create a lake the size of Manhattan 40 feet deep. Even today at the Savannah River facility in Georgia 180,000 gallons of radioactive and hazardous waste is discharged into seepage basins everyday.

Was HIV Genetically Engineered?

Even if HIV is not the only factor that causes AIDS, there exists a strong link between HIV and AIDS. Currently, there is evidence that shows that HIV may be the product of genetic engineering. In January 1986, the French-born and trained biologists, Professor Jakob and Dr. Lilli Segal, published a pamphlet, AIDS: USA-Home Made Evil; Not Imported from Africa, extensively reprinted in

English-speaking Africa. The scientists, a biophysicist and a biologist affiliated with the Humboldt University of Berlin, pointed out that examination of the genes making up HIV reveals that the differences between it and other retroviruses ostensibly in the same family "could not have come about by a natural way known to the biologist." They called the virus "a chimera, created only a few years ago," and they suggest Fort Detrick, Maryland, the site of much U.S. government CBW research, as the probable birthplace.

The Segals argue that HIV could not have evolved naturally from other members of the retrovirus family, but was rather assembled in a way which could only have occurred in a laboratory. They analyzed comparisons of HTLV-I with HTLV-III which indicated that the differences were "not of a magnitude to be explained by mutations. It was rather a matter of a complete restructuring, the disappearance of important structural parts and the emergence of new gene groups. A change from the HTLV-I to the HTLV-III could not have come about by a natural way known to the biologist."

"Green Monkey" Theory

The Segals also debunk the so-called "green monkey" theory, a theory supported by Dr. Gallo and a number of other researchers. (This theory posits that a simian retrovirus was transformed, or mutated, into the human retrovirus, after African victims were either bitten by the green monkey, or ate green monkey meat.) They explain convincingly that the minimal similarities found between simian T-lymphotropic virus III (STLV-III) found in some green monkeys and HTLV-III "is not surprising since we know that proteins of certain ranges of the virus are similar in all retroviruses." With virtually no serious testing or examination, the theory that AIDS may have arisen in the green monkey and then transferred to Africans--the first AIDS patients--was fed to credulous press which, as the Segals note,

99

"even reported that the two [retroviruses] could hardly be distinguished."

They also examined the epidemiology of the disease, and their views contrast strongly with Dr. Gallo's. Gallo states that the disease was first described in 1981 (although with the benefit of hindsight a number of cases dating to 1978 and 1979 were then recognizable as AIDS) and "is probably the results of a new infection of human beings that began in central Africa, perhaps as recently as the 1950s. From there it probably spread to the Caribbean and then to the U.S. and Europe.

Although the Segals agree with the dates of reported cases, they vigorously deny the suspected earlier origin in Africa. Moreover, they point out that the early cases, in New York, San Francisco, and Chicago, indicate an outbreak at least as early as 1979 in the U.S. And they stress, cases in western Europe and in Africa were only reported later.

Why Does AIDS Come From?

In A Survey of Chemical and Biological Warfare by Cookson and Nottingham, published in 1969, which documents the type of biological and chemical research and warfare being carried on in the Western World. Their work centered on chemical agents for riot control and the rise of biological agents as weapons that could be dispatch unexpectedly on the "enemy." This "scientific" research was/is being supported by the governments of the United States, Canada, Britain, and Germany. The crucial thing that the authors document is the early experimentation with viruses that would attack the immune system of people.

Dr. Theodore A. Strecker has unearthed evidence that the AIDS virus was created in a laboratory at Fort Detrick, Maryland from smallpox and hepatitis B vaccines. In Dr. Strecker's "The Strecker Memorandum" he asserts the following:

1) AIDS is a man-made disease.
2) AIDS is not a homosexual disease.
3) AIDS is not a venereal disease.
4) AIDS can be carried by mosquitoes.
5) Condoms will not prevent AIDS.[1]
6) There are at least six different AIDS viruses loose in the world.
7) There will never be a vaccine cure.
8) The AIDS virus was introduced into Africa by the World Health Organization (WHO).
9) The AIDS virus can live outside the body.

Dr. William Campbell Douglass, a fourth-generation physician and the National Health Federation's "Doctor of the Year" in 1987, agrees with Dr. Strecker's assertion that AIDS is man-made. In his book, AIDS: The End of Civilization, he states:

> The world was startled when the London Times reported on its front page, May 11, 1987, that the World Health Organization (WHO) had "triggered" the AIDS epidemic in Africa though the WHO smallpox immunization program. The only people in the free world not surprised by the London Times front page expose were the Americans--because they never heard about it. It is chilling to think that our press is so controlled that the most momentous news break since the assassination of President Kennedy didn't even make the sports section, much less the front page of any American daily paper, radio or television news.

According to the London Times of May 11, 1987 in an article, "Smallpox Vaccine Triggered AIDS Virus" by Pearce Wright:

---

[1]More than one out of every 200 condoms were found to be defective in laboratory test, a UCLA study has found. The defective condoms either allowed water or air to escape, failed strength tests or leaked the AIDS virus, the Los Angles Times reports.

Although no detailed figures are available, WHO information indicated that AIDS league table of Central Africa matches the concentration of vaccinations... The greatest spread of HIV infection coincides with the most intense immunization programmer, with the number of people immunized being as follows: Zaire 36,878,000; Zambia 19,060,000; Tanzania 14,972,000; Uganda 11,616,000; Malawi 8,118,000; Rwanda 3,382,000 and Burundi 3,274,000.

Pearce Wright also notes that Brazil was also "covered in the eradication campaign," and that about 14,000 Haitians on United Nations assignment to central Africa were also infected. Mr. Wright also states, "Charity and health workers are convinced that millions of new AIDS cases are about to hit southern Africa. After a meeting of fifty experts near Geneva this month it was revealed that up to 75,000,000, one-third of the population, could have the disease within the next five years." There have already been over 50,000 deaths in Africa from AIDS and with the possibility that up to 75 million African people may be infected, the 1990s will definitely be a period of chaotic change for that continent and the rest of the world.

CHAPTER 12

A NEW PATH

> A journey of a thousand miles must begin with a single step.
>
> Lao-tzu

In the first chapter, I mentioned quite a few times that Black people must seek a new path to achieve our liberation. Some of you may be wondering: What exactly is this new path? Well, to tell you the truth, I don't exactly know and even if I did claim to know, this is something that each person must, to a certain extent, figure out on her or his own. We should all be reminded of the speech given by Ikem Osodi, the protagonist of Chinua Achebe's *Anthills of the Savannah*:

> ...Give us the answer! Give us the answer! You know it was the same old cry heard by Jesus Christ from his lazy-minded, soft-brained, bread-hungry hangers-on in Galilee or Gardarene or wherever it was. Give us a miracle! Give us a miracle and we will believe in you. Cut out the parables and get to the point. Time is short! We want results! Now, now! No I cannot give you the answer you are clamouring for. Go home and think! I cannot decree your pet, text-book revolution. I want instead to excite general enlightenment by forcing all the people to examine the condition of their lives because, as the saying goes, the unexamined life is not worth living... As a writer I aspire

only to widen the scope of that self-examination. I don't want to foreclose it with a catchy, half-baked orthodoxy. My critics say: There is no time for your beautiful educational programme; the masses are ready and will be enlightened in the course of the struggle. And they quote Fanon on the sin of betraying the revolution. They do not realize that *revolutions are betrayed just as much by stupidity, incompetence, impatience and precipitate action as by doing nothing at all.* [Emphasis mine.]

To find that new path we all must "go home and think," self-examination and self-knowledge is essential. And when I speak of home I speak of Africa. We must realize that Africans have had empires, governments, constitutions, and "bills" of rights centuries before Europeans emerged from their caves. [See Appendix C, Ancient African Constitution and Fundamental Rights of African People.] Any path to liberation must include a thorough knowledge of our past glories and failures as a people.

Even though the path is not well-defined, there are still a number of things that are certain. One thing that is certain is that when we venture down any path we must be strong. When I speak of strength, I mean strong in all aspects: mentally, physically, and spiritually. We must become tigers!

Marcus Garvey And The Tiger Cub

One such tiger was Marcus Garvey. In 1923, when Marcus Garvey was famed on mail fraud charges the District Attorney appealed to the jury by crying out: "Gentlemen, will you let the tiger loose?" Marcus Garvey later responded in his last speech before he was incarcerated:

The tiger is already loose, and he has been at large for so long that it is no longer one tiger, but there are many tigers.... The world is

104

ignorant of the scope of this great movement, when it thinks that by laying low any one individual it can permanently silence this great spiritual wave, that has taken hold of the souls and the hearts and minds of 400,000,000 Negroes throughout the world. We have only started; we are just on our way; we have just made the first lap in the great race for existence, and for a place in the political and economic sun of men.

And over 65 years later and it still seems like we have just only started. When I look at the current state of Black people, I don't see enough tigers out there but I am reminded of a tale about a tiger cub that was raise by goats.

This cub only seeing goats all his life, he became like a goat, or as much like one as a tiger could. Then one day, after the tiger had begun to mature, the herd was attack by a fierce old male tiger. Discovering himself face to face with the terrible jungle being, the young tiger gazed at the apparition in amazement. The first moment passed; then he began to feel self-conscious. Uttering a forlorn bleat, he plucked a thin leaf of grass and chewed it, while the other stared.

Suddenly the mighty intruder demanded: "What are you doing here among these goats? What are chewing there?" The funny little creature bleated. The old one became really terrifying. He roared, "Why do you make this silly sound?" and before the other could respond, seized him roughly by the scruff and shook him, as though to knock him back to his senses.

Ultimately, the young tiger is led to discover his tigerhood. He arose and opened his mouth with a mighty yawn, just as though he were waking from a night of sleep - a night that had held him long under its spell, for years and years. Stretching his form, he arched his back, extending and spreading his paws. The tail lashed the ground, and suddenly from his throat there burst the terrifying, triumphant roar of a tiger.

The grim teacher, meanwhile, had been watching closely and with increasing satisfaction. The transformation had actually taken place. When the roar was finished he demanded gruffly: "Now do you know what you really are?"

Indeed, what are we Africans doing here among these goats? When I think of glorious past of Africa, I must demand: People, my people it's time that we wake up from our deep sleep, spit that grass out of our mouths, and begin to learn what we really are. We have to listen to and learn from those fierce old tigers in our midst, so that we will realize what we really are. Self-knowledge is definitely the key to our liberation, as the Kamitic (ancient Egyptian) saying goes: "Know yourself and you shall know god."

A Dream

Last night, in a dream, I sat down under a kola nut tree and had a chat with our noble ancestors. They revealed to me that it was indeed time for Africans to once again be the rulers of their own destiny. "For many generations our children and our children's children have forsaken us," they said, "they have followed the ways of the white man and we were forced to curse our own children. Now we see that some are once again beginning to hear our voices in the wind. Those who have responded to our voices shall lead our people out of the wilderness and the curse shall be lifted and the sun shall shine bright once again on the place that is now known as Africa."

In this dream I was reminded of a young Mandinke prince named Sundiata, the Hungering Lion. His entire royal family was executed by Sumanguru, King of the Sossos, in order that his rule over the Mandinkes would not be contested. Sundiata was spared because all the healers of the land had examined him and had declared him an incurable invalid. Sumanguru was certain that this cripple would never be a threat to him.

The legend of Sundiata tells how the young prince had fought against his disability. Through sheer determination, after months of effort, he was able to stand with a cane, then walk, then abandon his cane. His strength grew with his age. He earn fame as a hunter and horseman, and for his courage and knowledge of military life.

In 1230, Sundiata was named king of Mali and with the aid of an army loaned by a neighboring king, Sundiata moved into Mali to claim his throne. Once in Mali, he began preparing for the inevitable confrontation with Sumanguru. It was five years before the showdown took place and Sundiata was able to convincingly defeat and kill Sumanguru.

To me this bit of history has great significance to present day Africans. I believe it has great significance because all the leaders and healers in this land have declared that we Africans are today "incurable invalids" and unable to take control of our own destinies. Hence many of us are allow to stay around because we present no real threat. But some of us, through sheer determination are starting to stand up and walk like the man and woman we were meant to be. What will happen from here? Only time shall tell.

A Complete Education

In our search for the truth and knowledge it is imperative that we educate ourselves but we must be careful; much of what we come to know as "education" is nothing more than dogma and propaganda, designed to imprison our minds and protect us against the shafts of impartial evidence. So when I speak of education, I speak of a complete education, one that addresses the whole person: mind, body and spirit. We must transcend the mentality of: if we can just get more of that white man's "education" then things will get better. Of course we must strive for and achieve higher education but we also realize its limitations. We must

107

learn not to believe everything we told by professors and witch doctors.

If what you seek in life is only material comfort than maybe the job you will obtain as the result of your "education" will be sufficient; but if you seek more out of life than mere material comfort then: What good is your "education?" If you do not understand the legal, political, tax, or business systems of this nation, all of which have a tremendous capacity to oppress you. What good is your "education?" If you do not understand the principles of nutrition and physical fitness, and their importance in you leading a long and healthy life. What good is your "education?" If you do not have a positive image of yourself or your people. If Black people are to redeem themselves then our educational goal must be to strive for a complete education and not just some certificate or degree.

My own experience with education is some what reflected in the words of Oscar Wilde: "The only time my education was seriously interrupted was when I went to school." I probably received one of the best and well-rounded "education" that this nation's institutions could have provided. I graduated from the Bronx High School of Science which has a reputation of being one of the best high schools in the nation; I spent two years at the U.S. Naval Academy at Annapolis, where I was "educated" with a military twist; and I received a bachelor's degree from the University of Pennsylvania, an Ivy League school. And yet after I had finish attending all of these prestigious institutions, I soon found out how little I really did know. My education was (and still is) far from complete.

The fact that most people do not receive a complete education is no accident or simply a case of a lack of resources. For if you were to acquire a complete education then you would be forced to look inward and take responsibility for your own life. This is extremely threatening to the institutions that try to control your life, for it takes power away from the institutions and gives control back to the individual. The reason why you are denied a complete education is no different than the reason why slaves were not allow to learn how to read. Of course, as the needs of the institutions and society in general change, so does what is allow to be learned.

Why do you think that in a nation where there is suppose to existed a separation of church and state that some states refused to allow Darwin's theory of evolution to be taught in their school districts. It is not because they were such good Christians or were interested in the "truth"; it is because the ones who control the institution know that if you start to doubt one thing then maybe you might start doubting something else, then another thing and so on; and soon that institution begins to lose control. In short, you cannot expect the institutions (i.e., government, churches, corporations, etc.) that try to control your life to give you the education you need to make an informed decision. They would rather have you uneducated, in that way they will be able to do what any "proper" institution should do and that is make the "right" decisions for you.

As we struggle to obtain a complete education, will we gain a better focus on those forces that oppress us and we will begin to learn certain things: we will learn not to blame all white people for our oppression when the true source of our oppression lies within a small subset thereof; we will learn that our true oppressors are not so much the ones who call us "niggers" to our faces but the ones who shake our hands and pat us on the back for being "good boys and girls"; we will learn that the federal government is not our friend; we will learn that corporate America is not our friend; we will learn to love ourselves and come together as a people; we will learn not to hate, for hatred is the tool of the coward and a disease born of ignorance and fear; we will learn that we have the power to determine our destiny; we will learn that the American dream is nothing more than just one of many myths that are used to control us; and we will learn that beyond the myths of America our potential as a people will be boundless.

"Education" In The U.S.

According to my own primitive research, I would estimate that 99% of the people in U.S. is unaware of about 90% of the material covered in this book. Why are people unaware? Well, there is a theory known as the Theory of Cognitive Dissonance (TCD) which holds that the mind involuntarily rejects information not in line with previous thoughts and/or actions. The "education" you are given by schools and the media uses this principle to make sure that you stay unaware of what is really going on. I will even contend that the "educational" process in this country is so overwhelmingly successful that the vast majority of people after reading this book will reject totally this information or fail to grasp the true magnitude of the deception perpetrated by the "educational" process.

The average person would be completely shock how few people are persuaded by facts or impartial evidence. This is the main reason why a presidents like Ronald Reagan and George Bush are so popular. They make absolutely no pretense that they are telling the truth, they just say what the people want to hear. Following the 1984 vice-presidential debate this point was driven home by George Bush's press secretary, Peter Teeley, who told reporters: "You can say anything you want in a debate, and 80 million people hear it. If reporters then document that a candidate spoke untruthfully, so what? Maybe 200 people read it, or 2,000 or 20,000." (New York Times, October 19, 1984).

If things are so bad, as I claim, then why are so few people complaining? In ancient Rome they called it "panem et circenses" (bread and circuses). Today it's called welfare, social security, video games, sports and television. The provision of the means of life (if you can call it living) and recreation by government (and now also multi-national corporations) to appease discontent and distract the masses. The majority of the people in the United States are well fed, comfortable and amused, and it is difficult for them to conceive (recall the TCD) that the ones that control their government are engaged in a system of massive plunder and repression. More are starting to catch on as the manifestations, such as the S&L crisis, massive budget debt, inflation, bank failures, reduced funding of social programs, and police brutalities, of this system are coming to light.

Example Of Mis-Education

In the his-story we are taught, we learn that in 1066, William the Conqueror, Duke of Normandy, took between ten thousand and fifteen thousand knights across the English Channel and conquered a tiny island called England. But most of us never learn about a contemporary empire in West Africa called Ghana, which means place of the war chief. In the monumental *Book of Roads and Kingdoms*, published in 1067, Al Bekri, a Moorish geographer, described the Ghana of that time:

> The king who governs [Ghana] at present...is called Tenkaminen; Tenkaminen is the master of a large empire and a formidable power.... The king of Ghana can put two hundred thousand warriors in the field, more than forty thousand being armed with bow and arrow....
> When he gives audience to his people to listen to their complaints and set them to rights, he sits in a pavilion around which stand ten horses with gold- embroidered trappings. Behind the king stand ten pages holding shields and gold-mounted swords; on his right are the sons of princes of his empire, splendidly clad and with gold plaited in their hair. The governor of the city is seated on the ground in front of the king, and all around him

111

are seated his viziers. The door of the pavilion is guarded by dogs of an excellent breed who almost never leave the king's presence and who wear collars of gold and silver, ornamented with the same metals. The beginning of the royal audience is announced by the beating of a kind of drum which they call deba, made of a long piece of hollowed wood. The people gather when they hear the sound....

When Al Bekri's *Book* was published in 1067, Ghana had been standing for about seven hundred years and would stand for about hundred more.

Ancient Ghana acquired its strength and wealth from the movement of two precious minerals: gold from the south and salt from the north. Other commodities were also involve: copper and cotton goods, fine tools and swords from Arabian workshops and afterwards from Italy and Germany, horses from Barbary and Egypt, ivory and kola nuts and household slaves from the south; but the staples of the trade were always salt and gold.

The power of Ghana became legendary: writing in the twelfth century at the court of the Norman king Roger II of Sicily, al-Idrisi described how the lords of Ghana would often feed thousands at a time, spreading banquets more lavish than any had ever seen before.

Grown famous by its wealth, Ghana attracted rivals and invaders. After continually being attacked by various other nations and tribes, Ghana began to crumble and the last Ghanaian capital was lost in 1230. This brought to an end this once great West African empire.

Reflecting on Western His-story

Now, as I look back on the last few centuries, dominated by uninspiring materialistic western ideologies, I find it both amusing and disheartening that Blacks have been striving to be equal to white people. In the future Black people should never set our sights that low. The system we find ourselves under today teaches us a preoccupation with material benefits with little regard for spiritual costs. It would wise for us to pause and reevaluate our fundamental ideals and goals before we continue to give our allegiance to a system shaped by power and greed. Such systems are invariably self-destructive and primarily benefit only a small elite. In today's world, we are faced with: increasing poverty, hunger, and homelessness; an AIDS pandemic; drug abuse; crime; teenage pregnancy; the decay of the family structure; racial, ethic, and religious conflicts; ozone depletion; the greenhouse effect; acid rain; decreasing biological diversity; deforestation and desertification; smog; unsafe drinking water; oil spills; toxic and hazardous waste. So it does not take a genius to conclude that something is definitely awry with the system in which we live. When we consider all the problems in the world, we must keep in mind that in our fight against oppression, we must not whole-heartily accept Western values. Instead, we must reflect on our culture and heritage, and we will realize that integrity, dignity, tolerance, and compassion are values that are more important than greed, domination, and the acquisition of power.

When I think of the future of Black people there is one thing that I am absolutely sure of - if we stay on our current course with our current so-called leaders we will never overcome our present status as a subjugated people. Integration (just simply being allow around white people) or Civil Rights (the "legal" fact that we are able to do anything that anyone else is able to do) is not going to solve our problems or make us happy as a people. The dream of Dr. Martin Luther King, Jr. is indeed a beautiful and noble dream but just like the Christian doctrine that it is based upon, it has not stood the test of time in the harsh world of reality. It has been more than a quarter of a century since Dr. King proclaimed his dream and it does not look any closer to reality today than it did on that memorable day in 1963. According to one study done in 1990 by the National Opinion Research Center: 3 of 4 whites surveyed believe that black people are more likely than whites to prefer living on welfare; 62% of whites believe that blacks are more likely to be lazy; and 53% believe blacks are less intelligent. We will never seem equal in the eyes of white people as long as we are contented to remain a subjugated people and allow white people to dictate what is best for us.

Christianity

As for Christianity, it has been the major religion of the Western world for almost two thousand years and yet the Western World has been cause of all of the worst man-induced catastrophe in the world: World War I, where over 20 million people died; World War II, where over 16 million people died (over 100,000 [mostly woman and children] in one day when then the U.S. dropped the Atomic bomb on Hiroshima); the Holy Inquisition, where millions of "heretics" were burned to the stake at the hands of the Roman Catholic Church, a practice that continued for over 600 years and didn't end until the 19th century; the African Slave Trade, where as many as 250 million African died over a period of over three and half centuries; the almost complete extinction of the indigenous people of three continents (North America, South America, and Oceania [Australia and New Zealand]); the execution of millions of Jewish people and other "undesirables"; the polluted condition of the environment, which is causing millions of people world-wide to die prematurely; AIDS, which has already killed over 200,000 people world-wide and is continuing to spread; and the list goes on. With such a dubious history, Black people would either be complete fools or complete idiots to continue to entrust our fate, our children's fate, or our children's children's fate in the hands of white people.

A Reevaluation Of Western Domination

When dealing with the subject of Western domination, I think that it is very important that we realize how brief this period has actually been when taken in the context of the entire span of human civilization. The Africans were the first men and women on this earth and the first to be civilize. Africans were civilized and built great structures like the pyramids many thousands of years before the Europeans emerged from their caves. The only reason Europeans were able to dominate the rest of world is because while the rest of world was trying to build better societies to enable them to live in harmony with their environment, Europeans were busy working on more efficient ways to kill and destroy. Europeans are able to dominate not because they are more intelligent than any one else but because they are extremely violent.

One prime example of this behavior is the European use of gunpowder. The Chinese were using gunpowder for hundreds of years before the Europeans even knew what the stuff was. Yet, the Chinese didn't used gunpowder as a weapon. This is not because the Chinese were stupid, on contrary Chinese civilization at this time was far more advanced than European civilization. For the Chinese and the rest of the non-white world thinking of more efficient ways to kill your enemy was against their teachings of what a warrior should be. Warriors were suppose to be brave and strong, only a coward or a psychotic would think of more efficient ways to kill another human being.

Even with the advanced killing technology of the Europeans the old states of Black Africa didn't just surrender. One outstanding fact about the old states of Black Africa, well understood in earlier times but today forgotten, is that they were seldom or never conquered from outside the continent. They resisted invasion. They remained inviolate. Only here and there along the coast could European men-at-arms gain foothold even when they tried to win more. The Arabo-Berber states of northern Africa also had little luck with their overland invasions of the south, and were in the end frustrated and forced to withdraw.

Writers of the colonial period were prone to explain this fact of successful African resistance by reference to the climate and the mosquito. Certainly, malaria and the sun were grim discourages of foreign invasion. Yet the early records indicate another and more persuasive safeguard against conquest. They point to the striking power of African armies. They show that it was the military factor, time and again, which prove decisive.

"With nauseating presumption," complained Father Cavazzi of northern Angola in 1687, "these nations think themselves the foremost men in the world, and nothing will persuade them to the contrary.... They imagine that Africa is not only the greatest part of the world, but also the happiest and most agreeable." The ruling lords, he found, were even more arrogant. "Similar opinions are held by the king himself, but in a manner still more remarkable. For he is persuaded that there is no other monarch in the world who is his equal, or exceeds him in power or the abundance of wealth..."

The Future Of Africans

Knowledge is Power! United we stand, divided we fall! These statements may sound a little corny but nevertheless they still hold true. If we holdfast to our principles, then the future of Africans, those at home and those abroad, will be ours and ours alone to determine. The near future is going to produce some difficult and chaotic times for all the peoples of the world. The world we know today is going to look much different in just a few years. We are living in a pressure cooker and it is about to explode. If we just sit around playing with ourselves then we will only become pitiful victims of the crises yet to come. History clearly demonstrates that times of chaos doesn't necessarily mean disaster; they also provide opportunities for those with vision enough to prepare for them.

If we are going to survive the chaotic times ahead then Africans must realize who are enemies are. For the most part our enemies are white people but many of our enemies look like us. Once we realize who are enemies then we will be able to take advantage of the next opportunity for liberation that will soon come.

What opportunity? Well, the African in America has had many opportunities for liberation but we just chose to fight the wrong enemy. The Civil War, World War I, and World War II were all opportunities that we Africans failed to capitalize on. In future such conflicts, our best option will be to stay on the sidelines and just let white people kill each other off (this stand is only fair because that is exactly the stand white people take with regards to us). When both sides is at its weakest that is the time when we should strike out for our liberation.

With the rise of fascism in the United States and Europe, there is definitely going to be a powerplay and a fight for power which will result in the next great war. The war against Iraq was just target practice for the American War Machine compared to war yet to come. Good men (good only in the sense that they will fight and kill other white people) like Hitler, Mussolini, and Stalin will rise once again and kill many of their own people to secure power. And once again, because we have always been good attack dogs, we will be ask to fight such men. If we really want to be free we will refuse to fight and tell them to fight their own damn wars! Then when both sides are weak and weary of fighting that will be our call to battle. Once victory is obtain, the curse of the ancestors will be lifted and the sun will once again shine bright on the place that is know called Africa.

PROTOCOL OF ZION NO. 1

...Putting aside fine phrases we shall speak of the significance of each thought: by comparisons and deductions we shall throw light upon surrounding facts.

What I am about to set forth, then, is our system from the two point of view, that of ourselves and that of the goyim (i.e., non-Jews).

It must be noted that men with bad instincts are more in number than the good, and therefore the best results in governing them are attained by violence and terrorization, and not by academic discussions. Every man aims at power, everyone would like to become a dictator if only he could, and rare indeed are the men who would not be willing to sacrifice the welfare of all for the sake of securing their own welfare.

What has restrained the beasts of prey who are called men? What has served for their guidance hitherto?

In the beginnings of the structure of society they were subjected to brutal and blind force; afterwards - to Law, which is the same force only disguised. I draw the conclusion that by the law of nature right lies in force.

Political freedom is an idea but not a fact. This idea one must know how to apply whenever it appears necessary with this bait of an idea to attract the masses of the people to one's party for the purpose of crushing another who is in authority. This task is rendered easier if the opponent has himself been infected with the ideas of freedom, so-called liberalism, and, for the sake of an idea, is willing to yield some of his power. It is precisely here that the triumph of our theory appears: the slackened reins of government are immediately, by the law of life, caught up and gathered together by a new hand, because the blind might of the nation cannot for one single day exist without guidance, and the new authority merely fits into the place of the old already weakened by liberalism.

In our day the power which has replaced that of the rulers who were liberal is the power of Gold. Time was when Faith ruled. The idea of freedom is impossible of realization because no one knows how to use it with moderation. It is enough to hand over a people to self-government for a certain length of time for that people to be turned into a disorganized mob. From that moment on we get internecine strife which soon develops into battles between classes, in the midst of which States burn down and their importance is reduced to that of a heap of ashes.

Whether a State exhausts itself in its own convulsions, whether its internal discord brings it under the power of external foes - in any case it can be accounted irretrievably lost: it is in our power. The despotism of Capital, which is entirely in our hands, reaches out to it a straw that the State, willy-nilly, must take hold of: if not - it goes to the bottom.

Should anyone of a liberal mind say that such reflections as the above are immoral I would put the following questions: - If every State has two foes and if in regard to the external foe it is allowed and not considered immoral to use every manner and art of conflict, as for example to keep the enemy in ignorance of plans of attack and defense, to attack him by night or in superior numbers, then in what way can the same means in regard to a worse foe, the destroyer of the structure of society and the commonweal, be called immoral and not permissible?

Is it possible for any sound logical mind to hope with any success to guide crowds by the aid of reasonable counsels and arguments, when any objection or contradiction, senseless though it may be, can be made and when such objection may find more favor with the people, whose powers of reasoning are superficial? Men in masses and the men of the masses, being guided solely by petty passions, paltry beliefs, customs, traditions and sentimental theorism, fall prey to party dissension,

119

which hinders any kind of agreement even on the basis of a perfectly reasonable argument. Every resolution of a crowd depends upon a chance or packed majority, which in its ignorance of political secrets, put forth some ridiculous resolution that lays in the administration a seed of anarchy.

The political has nothing in common with the moral. The ruler who is governed by the moral is not a skilled politician, and is therefore unstable on his throne. He who wishes to rule must have recourse both to cunning and to make-believe. Great national qualities, like frankness and honesty, are vices in politics, for they bring down rulers from their thrones more effectively and more certainly than the most powerful enemy. Such qualities must be the attributes of the kingdoms of the goyim, but we must in no wise be guided by them.

Our right lies in force. The word "right" is an abstract thought and proved by nothing. The word means no more than: - Give me what I want in order that thereby I may have proof that I am stronger than you.

Where does right begin? Where does it end?

In any State in which there is a bad organization of authority, an impersonality of laws and of the rulers who have lost their impersonality of laws and of the rulers who have lost their personality amid the flood of rights ever multiplying out of liberalism, I find a new right - to attack by the right of the strong, and to scatter to the winds all existing forces of order and regulation, to reconstruct all institutions and to become the sovereign lord of those who have left to us the rights of their power by laying them down voluntarily in their liberalism.

Our power in the present tottering condition of all forms of power will be more invisible until the moment when it has gained such strength that no cunning can any longer undermine it.

Out of the temporary evil we are now compelled to commit will emerge the good of an unshakeable rule, which will restore the regular course of the machinery of the national life, brought to naught by liberalism. The result justifies the means. Let us, however, in our plans, direct our attention not so much to what is good and moral as to what is necessary and useful.

Before us is plan in which is laid down strategically the line from which we cannot deviate without running the risk of seeing the labor of many centuries brought to naught.

In order to elaborate satisfactory forms of action it is necessary to have regard to the rascality, the slackness, the instability of the mob, its lack of capacity to understand and respect the conditions of its own life, or its own welfare. It must be understood that the might of a mob is blind, senseless and unreasoning force ever at the mercy of a suggestion from any side. The blind cannot lead the blind without bringing them into the abyss; consequently, members of the mob, upstarts from the people even though they should be a genius for wisdom, yet having no understanding of the political, cannot come forward as leaders of the mob without bringing the whole nation to ruin.

Only one trained from childhood for independent rule can have understanding of the words that can be made up of the political alphabet.

A people left to itself i.e., to upstarts from its midst brings itself to ruin by party dissensions excited by the pursuit of power and honors and the disorders arising therefrom. Is it possible for the masses of the people calmly and without petty jealousies to form judgments, to deal with the affairs of the country, which cannot be mixed up with personal interests? Can they defend themselves from an external foe? It is unthinkable, for a plan broken up into as many parts as there are heads in the mob, loses all homogeneity, and thereby becomes unintelligible and impossible of execution.

It is only with a despotic ruler that plans can be elaborated extensively and clearly in such a way as to distribute the whole properly among the several parts of the machinery of the State: from this the conclusion is inevitable that a satisfactory form of government for any country is one that concentrates in the hands of one responsible person. Without an absolute despotism there can be no existence for civilization which is carried on not by the masses but by their guide, whosoever that person may be. The mob is a savage and displays its savagery at every opportunity. The moment the mob seizes freedom in its hands it quickly turns to anarchy, which in itself is highest degree of savagery.

Behold the alcoholized animals, bemused with drink, the right to an immoderate use of which comes along with freedom. It is not for us and ours to walk that road. The peoples of the goyim are bemused with alcoholic liquors; their youth has grown stupid on classicism and from early immorality, into which it has been inducted by our special agents - by tutors, lackeys, governesses in the houses of the wealthy, by clerks and others, by our women in the places of dissipation frequented by the goyim. In the number of these last I count also the so-called "society ladies," voluntary followers of the others in corruption and luxury.

Our countersign is - Force and Make-believe. Only force conquers in political affairs, especially if it be concealed in the talents essential to statesmen. Violence must be the principle, and cunning and make-believe the rule for governments which do not want to lay down their crowns at the feet of agents of some new power. This evil is the one and only means to attain the end, the good. Therefore we must not stop at bribery, deceit and treachery when they should serve towards the attainment of our end. In politics one must know how to seize the property of others without hesitation if by it we secure submission and sovereignty.

Our State, marching along the path of peaceful conquest, has the right to replace the horrors of war by less noticeable and more satisfactory sentences of death, necessary to maintain terror which tends to produce blind submission. Just but merciless severity is the greatest factor of strength in the State: not only for the sake of gain but also in the name of duty, for the sake of victory, we must keep to the programme of violence and make-believe. The doctrine of squaring accounts is precisely as strong as the means of which it makes use. Therefore it is not so much by the means themselves as by the doctrine of severity that we shall triumph and bring all governments into subjection to our super-government. It is enough for them to know that we are merciless for all disobedience to cease.

Far back in ancient times we were the first to cry among the masses of the people the words "Liberty, Equality, Fraternity," words many times repeated since those days by stupid poll-parrots who from all sides round flew down upon these baits and with them carried away the well-being of the world, true freedom of the individual, formerly so well guarded against the pressure of the mob. The would-be wise men of the goyim, the intellectuals, could not make anything out of the uttered words in their abstractness; did not note the contradiction of their meaning and inter-relation: did not see that in nature there is no equality, cannot be freedom; that Nature herself has established inequalities of minds, of characters, and capacities, just as immutably as she has established subordination to her laws: never stopped to think that the mob is a blind thing, that upstarts elected from among it to bear rule are, in regard to the political, the same blind men as the mob itself, that the adept, though he be a fool, can yet rule, whereas the non-adept, even if he were a genius, understands nothing in the political - to all these things the goyim paid no regard; yet all the time it was based upon these things that dynastic rule rested: the father passed on to the son a knowledge of the course of political affairs in such wise that none should know it but members of the dynasty and none could betray it to the governed. As time went on the meaning of the dynastic transference of the true position of affairs in the political was lost, and this aided the success of our cause.

In all corners of the earth the words "Liberty, Equality, Fraternity" brought to our ranks, thanks to our blind agents, whole legions who bore our banners with enthusiasm. And all the time these words were canker-worms at work boring into the well-being of the goyim, putting an end everywhere to peace, quiet, solidarity and destroying all the foundations of the goya States. As you will see later, this helped us to our triumph; it gave us the possibility, amount other things, of getting into our hands the master card - the destruction of privileges, or in other words of the very existence of the aristocracy of the goyim, that class which was the only defense peoples and countries had against us. On the ruins of the natural and genealogical aristocracy of the goyim we have set up the aristocracy of our educated class headed by the aristocracy of money. The qualifications for this aristocracy we have established in wealth, which is dependent upon us, and in knowledge, for which our learned elders provide the motive force.

Our triumph has been rendered easier by the fact that in our relations with the men whom we wanted we have always worked upon the most sensitive chords of the human mind, upon the cash account, upon the cupidity, upon the insatiability for material needs of man; and each one of these human weaknesses, taken alone, is sufficient to paralyze initiative, for it hands over the will of men to the disposition of him who has brought their activities.

The abstraction of freedom has enabled us to persuade the mob in all countries that their government is nothing but the steward of the people who are the owners of the country, and that the steward may be replaced like a worn-out glove.

It is this possibility of replacing the representatives of the people which has placed them at our disposal, and,as it were, given us the power of appointment.

SAC, Albany   August 25, 1967

<u>PERSONAL ATTENTION TO ALL OFFICES</u>

Director, FBI

 COUNTERINTELLIGENCE PROGRAM
 BLACK NATIONALIST - HATE GROUPS
 INTERNAL SECURITY

 ...The purpose of this new counterintelligence
endeavor is to expose, disrupt, misdirect, discredit,
or otherwise neutralize the activities of black
nationalist hate-type organizations and groupings,
their leadership, spokesmen, membership, and supporters, and to counter their propensity for violence
and civil disorder. The activities of all such groups
of intelligence interest to the Bureau must be followed
on a continuous basis so we will be in a position to
promptly take advantage of all opportunities for
counterintelligence and to inspire action in instances
where circumstances warrant. The pernicious background
of such groups, their duplicity, and devious maneuvers
must be exposed to public scrutiny where such publicity
will have a neutralizing effect. Efforts of the various
groups to consolidate their forces or to recruit new or
youthful adherents must be frustrated. No opportunity
should be missed to exploit through counterintelligence
techniques the organizational and personal conflicts of
the leaderships of the groups and where possible an effort should be made to capitalize upon existing conflicts between competing black nationalist
organizations. When an opportunity is apparent to disrupt or neutralize black nationalist, hate-type organizations through the cooperation of established
local news media contacts or through such contact with
sources available to the Seat of Government, in every
instance careful attention must be given to the
proposal to insure the targeted group is disrupted,
ridiculed, or discredited through the publicity and not
merely publicized....

 You are also cautioned that the nature of this
new endeavor is such that under no circumstances should
the existence of the program be made known outside the
Bureau and appropriate within-office security should be
afforded to sensitive operations and techniques considered under the program.

 <u>No counterintelligence action under this program may be initiated by the field without specific
prior Bureau authorization.</u>

BACKGROUND

...The Revolutionary Action Movement (RAM), a pro-Chinese communist group, was active in Philadelphia, Pa., in the summer of 1967. The Philadelphia Office alerted local police, who the put RAM leaders under close scrutiny. They were arrested on every possible charge until they could no longer make bail. As a result, RAM leaders spent most of the summer in jail and no violence traceable to RAM took place. ...

GOALS

For maximum effectiveness of the Counterintelligence Program, and to prevent wasted effort, long-range goals are being set.

1. Prevent the <u>coalition</u> of militant black nationalist groups. In unity there is strength; a truism that is no less valid for all its triteness. An effective coalition of black nationalist groups might be the first step toward a real "Mau Mau" in America, the beginning of a true black revolution.

2. Prevent the <u>rise of a "messiah"</u> who could unify, and electrify, the militant black nationalist movement. Malcolm X might have been such a "messiah;" he is the martyr of the movement today. Martin Luther King, Stokely Carmichael and Elijah Muhammed all aspire to this position. Elijah Muhammed is less of a threat because of his age. King could be a very real contender for this position should he abandon his supposed "obedience" to "white, liberal doctrines" (nonviolence) and embrace black nationalism. Carmichael has the necessary charisma to be a real threat in this way.

3. Prevent <u>violence</u> on the part of black nationalist groups. This is of primary importance, and is, of course, a goal of our investigative activity; it should also be a goal of the Counterintelligence Program. Through counterintelligence it should be possible to pinpoint potential troublemakers and neutralize them before they exercise their potential for violence.

4. Prevent militant black nationalist groups and leaders from gaining <u>respectability</u>, by discrediting them to three separate segments of the community. The goal of discrediting black nationalist must be

126

handled tactically in three ways. You must discredit those groups and individuals to, first, the responsible Negro community. Second, they must be discredited to the white community, both the responsible community and to "liberals" who have vestiges of sympathy for militant black nationalist(s) simply because they are Negroes. Third, these groups must be discredited in the eyes of Negro radicals, the followers of the movement. This last area requires entirely different tactics from the first two. Publicity about violent tendencies and radical statements merely enhances black nationalists to the last group; it adds "respectability" in a different way.

5. A final goal should be to prevent the long-range _growth_ of militant black nationalist organizations, especially among youth. Specific tactics to prevent these groups from converting young people must be developed. ...

TARGETS

Primary targets of the Counterintelligence Program, Black Nationalist-Hate Groups, should be the most violent and radical groups and their leaders. We should emphasize those leaders and organizations that are nationwide in scope and are most capable of disrupting this country. These targets should include the radical and violence-prone leaders, members, and followers of the:

Student Nonviolent Coordinating Committee (SNCC)
Southern Christian Leadership Conference (SCLC)
Revolutionary Action Movement (RAM)
Nation of Islam (NOI)

Offices handling these cases and those of Stokely Carmichael of SNCC, H. Rap Brown of SNCC, Martin Luther King of SCLC, Maxwell Stanford of RAM, and Elijah Muhammed of NOI, should be alert for counterintelligence suggestions. ...

SOME POLITICAL THEORIES AND PRINCIPLES OF ANCIENT AFRICAN CONSTITUTIONAL LAW AND THE FUNDAMENTAL RIGHTS OF THE AFRICAN PEOPLE

(Drawn from African Traditional Constitutional and Customary Laws. Different versions and modifications of the same laws occurred in different societies. From Chancellor Williams' *The Destruction of Black Civilization*)

I. The People are the first and final source of all power.

II. The rights of the community of people are, and of right ought to be, superior to those of any individual, including Chiefs and Kings (a) *The Will of the People* is the supreme law; (b) Chiefs and Kings are under the law, not above it.

III. Kings, Chiefs and Elders are *leaders*, not rulers. They are the elected representatives of the people and the instruments for executing their will.

IV. Government and people are one and the same.

V. The family is recognized as the primary social, judicial, economic and political unity in the society; the family council may function as a court empowered to try all internal (non-serious) matters involving only members of the Extended Family Group.

VI. The Elder of each Extended Family or Clan is its chosen representative of the Council.

VII. Decisions in council are made by the Elders. The Chief or King must remain silent. Even when the Council's decision is announced, it is through a Speaker (Linguist). Decrees or laws are issued in the same manner to assure that the voice of the Chief or King is the "voice of the people." (This is an example of a provision that had wide variations.)

VIII. The land belongs to no one. It is God's gift to mankind for use and sacred heritage, transmitted by our forefathers as a bond between the living and the dead, to be held in trust by each generation for the unborn who will follow, and thus to the last generation.

IX. Each family, therefore, has a right to land, free of charge, sufficient in acreage for its economic well-being; for the right to the opportunity and means to make a living is the right to live.

(a) The land, accordingly, cannot be sold or given away.

(b) The land may be held for life and passed on to the family's heirs, so on forever.

(c) The Chief is the Custodian of all land, the principal duty being to assure fair distribution and actual use.

X. All moneys, gifts, taxes and other forms of donations to Chief or King still belong to the people for relief or aid to individuals in times of need.

XI. Every member of the state has the right of appeal from a lower to higher court. (In some states appeal could be taken even from the King's Court to the "Mother of the Nation.")

(a) The procedure was from the Chief's Village Court to the District Court, to the Provincial Court, to the King's Court.

(b) Such appeals were allowed in serious or major crimes only (those affecting the whole society).

XII. Fines for offenses against an individual went to the victim, not the court.

(a) Part of the money received from the loser was returned to him as an expression of goodwill and desire for renewal of friendship.

(b) Another part was given as a fee to the trial court as an appreciation of justice.

XIII. "Royalty" in African terms means *Royal Worth*, the highest in character, wisdom, sense of justice and courage.

(a) He who founded the nation by uniting many as one must be the real leader, guide and servant of his people.

(b) The people, in honor of the founder of the nation, thereafter will elect Chiefs from the founder's family (lineage) if the heirs meet the original test that reflected the Founder's character, whose spirit was supposed to be inherited.

XIV. The trouble of one is the trouble of all. No one may go in want while others have anything to give. All are brothers and sisters. Each is his "brothers' or sisters' keeper."

XV. Age grades, sets, and classes are social, economic, political and military systems for (1) basic and advanced traditional education (formal); (2) individual and group responsibility roles; (3) police and military training; (4) division of labor; (5) rites of passage and social activities. In chiefless societies the age grades are the organs of social, economic and
political action.

XVI. Bride Price or Bride Wealth is the gift that signifies mutual acceptance on the part of both families and is intended as a family security bond which may be returned in part if the wife turns out to be worthless or utterly unsatisfactory. (Bride Wealth tended to stabilize the institution of marriage. This was not "wife-buying.")

XVII. The community as a whole is conceived of as *One Party*, opposition being conducted by leaders of various factions.

(1) Factions of opposition are usually formed by the different age-groups:

(2) Debates may go on indefinitely or until a consensus is reached.

(3) Once a consensus is reached, and the community's will determined, all open opposition to the common will must cease.

(4) Those whose opposition is so serious that they are unwilling to accept the new law may "splinter off' either individually or in

groups under a leader (to form a new state or the nucleus for it).

XVII.   In warfare the object is not to kill the enemy, but to overcome him with fear, if possible, such as screaming war cries, loud noise, hideously masked faces, etc. Where killing is unavoidable it must be kept at a minimum. In case of defeat there must be some kind of ruse to enable the enemy to retire in honor.

XIX. The African religion, not being a creed or "articles of faith," but an actual way of thinking and living, is reflected in all institutions and is, therefore, of the greatest constitutional significance.

(1) Politically, the role of the Chief as High Priest who presents the prayers of the people to his and their ancestors in Heaven, is the real source of his influence, political or otherwise.

(2) Socially, the "rites of passage," songs, and the dances (to drive away evil, etc.), as well as the purification and sacrificial rites for the atonement of sins-are important.

XX. Since religious and moral law must prevail and the race survive, a man may have more than one wife; for he is forbidden to sleep or cohabit with his wife either during the nine months of pregnancy or during the suckling period of one or two years thereafter. (1) The wife may not prepare meals for the husband or family during the menstrual period. (2) The husband is strictly forbidden to have any kind of relationship with one wife during the set period that belongs to another wife.

XXI. The supreme command of the fighting forces is under the Council, not the King. If the King becomes the Commander-in-Chief, it is through election by the Council because of his qualification as a general or field commander. This position ends with the war and the arm forces return to former status under the Council or, more directly under the respective Paramount chiefs. There were no standing armies.

131

THE FUNDAMENTAL RIGHTS
OF THE AFRICAN PEOPLE

The following is a representative number of human rights; also drawn
from customary laws or tradition constitutions:

Every member of the community had -
(1)   The right to equal protection of the law.
(2)   The right to a home.
(3)   The right to land sufficient for earning livelihood for oneself and family.
(4)   The right to aid in times of trouble.
(5)   The right to petition for redress of grievances.
(6)   The right to criticize and condemn any acts by the authorities or proposed new laws. (Opposition groups, in some areas called "The Youngmen," were recognized by law.)
(7)   The right to reject the community's final decision on any matter and to withdraw from the community unmolested - the right of rebellion and withdrawal.
(8)   The right to a fair trail. There must be no punishment greater than the offense, or fines beyond ability to pay. This latter is determined by income and status of the individual and his family.
(9)   The right to indemnity for injuries or loss caused by others.
(10) The right to family or community care in cases of sickness or accidents.
(11) The right to special aid from the Chief in circumstances beyond a family's ability.
(12) The right to a general education covering morals and good manners, family rights and responsibilities, kinship groups and social organization, neighborhoods and boundaries, farming and marketing, rapid mental calculation, and family, clan, tribal and state histories.
(13) The right to apprentice training for a useful vocation.

132

(14) The right to an inheritance as defined by custom.

(15) The right to develop one's ability and exercise any developed skills.

(16) The right to protect one's family and kinsmen, even by violent means if such becomes necessary and can be justified.

(17) The right to the protection of moral law in respect to wife and children - a right which not even the king can violate.

(18) The right of a man, even a slave, to rise to occupy the highest positions in the state if he has the requisite ability and character.

(19) The right to protection and treatment as a guest in enemy territory once one is within the gates of the enemy's village, town or city.

(20) And the right to an equal share in all benefits from common community undertakings if one has contributed to the fullest extent of his ability, no matter who or how many were able to contribute more.

Achebe, Chinua. *Anthills of the Savannah.* Doubleday, New York, 1987.

Adelman, Bob. "The Federal Reserve System: Creature of a Triumphant International Banking Establishment." *Bulletin: Committee to Restore the Constitution.* February 1989.

Alvarez, Robert, and Makhijani, Arjun. "Radioactive Waste: Hidden Legacy of the Arms Race." *Technology Review.* pp. 42-51, August/September 1988.

Beinin, Joel. "Origins of the Gulf War." *Open Magazine Pamphlet Series,* February 19, 1991.

Berger, Roman. "Who Deals Drug?" *Covert Action Information Bulletin.* pp. 17-18, Number 28 (Summer 1987).

Bielski, Vince, and Berstein, Dennis. "The Cocaine Connection." *Covert Action Information Bulletin.* pp. 13-16, Number 28 (Summer 1987).

Chernow, Ron. *The House of Morgan: An American Banking Dynasty and the Rise of Modern Finance.* Atlantic Monthly Press, New York, 1990.

Chomsky, Noam. "The New World Order." *Open Magazine Pamphlet Series,* March 1991.

_____. "On U.S. Gulf Policy." *Open Magazine Pamphlet Series,* February 5, 1991.

Domhoff, G. William. *Who Rules America Now?* Simon & Schuster, New York, 1983.

Garvey, Amy Jacques, ed. T*he Philosophy & Opinions of Marcus Garvey: Or, Africa for the Africans.* Majority Press, Dover, MA, 1923.

Glick, Brain. *War at Home: Covert Action Against U.S. Activists and What We Can Do About It.* South End Press, Boston, 1989.

Hatch, Richard. "Drugs, Politics, and Disinformation." *Covert Action Information Bulletin.* pp. 23-27, Number 28 (Summer 1987).

Hulet, Craig. "The Secret U.S. Agenda in the Gulf War." *Open Magazine Pamphlet Series,* March 6, 1991.

Huxley Aldous. *Brave New World*. Bantam Books, New York, 1967.

Jones, James H. *Bad Blood: The Tuskegee Syphilis Experiment - a Tragedy of Race and Medicine*. The Free Press, 1981.

Lappe, Frances Moore and Collins, Joseph. *Food First: Beyond The Myth of Scarcity*. Ballantine Books, New York, 1978.

Lawrence, Ken. "The Real Task of the CIA Remains Covert Action." *Covert Action Information Bulletin*. pp. 5-7, Number 35 (Fall 1990).

Lean, Geoffrey; Hinrichsen, Don and Markham, Adam. Prentice Hall Press, New York, 1990.

Lederer, Robert. "Chemical-Biological Warfare, Medical Experiments, and Population Control." *Covert Action Information Bulletin*. pp. 33-42, Number 28 (Summer 1987).

Lehrman, Nathaniel S. "Is AIDS Non-Infectious?: The Possibility and its CBW Implications." *Covert Action Information Bulletin*. pp. 55-62, Number 28 (Summer 1987).

MacMicheal, David. "The Other Iran-contra Cases." *Covert Action Information Bulletin*. pp. 52-55, Number 35 (Summer 1990).

Madhubuti, Haki R. *Enemies: The Clash of Races*. Third World Press, Chicago, 1978.

_____. *Black Men: Obsolete, Single, Dangerous? The Afikan American Family in Transition: Essays in Discovery, Solution, and Hope*. Third World Press, Chicago, 1990.

Marchetti, Victor, and Marks, John D. *The CIA and the Cult of Intelligence*. Dell, New York, 1974.

Nkrumah, Kwame. *Neo-Colonialism: The Last Stage of Imperialism*. International Publishers, New York, 1966.

Orwell, George. *1984*. Harcourt Brace Jovanovich, New York, 1949.

Quigley, Carroll. *The Anglo-American Establishment*. Books in Focus, New York, 1981.

_____. *Tragedy and Hope: A History of the World in our Time*. Macmillan Company, New York, 1966.

Ritter, E.A. *Shaka Zulu*. Penguin Books, New York, 1955.

Roberts, Archibald E. *The Most Secret Science*. Betty Ross Press, Fort Collins, CO, 1984.

Schoenman, Ralph. *Iraq and Kuwait: A History Suppressed*. Veritas Press, Santa Barbara, CA, 1990.

Sklar, Holly. *Reagan, Trilateralism and the Neoliberals: Containment and Intervention in the 1980s*. South End Press, Boston, 1986.

_____, ed. *Trilateralism: The Trilateral Commission and Elite Planning for World Management*. South End Press, Boston, 1980.

Stockwell, John. *In Search of Enemies: A CIA Story*. W. W. Norton & Company, New York, 1978.

_____. "Wartime Interview: U.S. Policy: The Need for War." *Open Magazine Pamphlet Series*, February 1, 1991.

Truong, David. "Running Drugs and Secret Wars." *Covert Action Information Bulletin*. pp. 3-5, Number 28 (Summer 1987).

Williams, Chancellor. *The Destruction of Black Civilization: Great Issues of a Race from 4500 B.C. to 2000 A.D.* Third World Press, Chicago, 1987.

When in the course of human events, it becomes necessary for one people to dissolve the political bands which have connected them with another, and to assume among the powers of the earth, the separate and equal station to which the Laws of Nature and of Nature's God entitle them, a decent respect to the opinions of mankind requires that they should declare the causes which impel them to the separation.-

We hold these truths to be self-evident, that all men are created equal, that they are endowed by their Creator with certain unalienable Rights, that among these are Life, Liberty and the pursuit of Happiness.-

That to secure these rights, Government are instituted among Men, deriving their just powers from the consent of the governed,-

That whenever any Form of Government becomes destructive of these ends, IT IS THE RIGHT OF THE PEOPLE TO ALTER OR ABOLISH IT, and to institute new Government, laying its foundation on such principles and organizing its powers in such form, as to them shall seem most likely to effect their Safety and Happiness. Prudence, indeed will dictate that Government long established should not be changed for light and transient causes; and accordingly all experience hath shown, that mankind are more disposed to suffer, while evils are sufferable, than to right themselves by abolishing the forms to which they are accustomed. But when a long train of abuses and usurpations, pursuing invariably the same Object evinces a design to reduce them under absolute Despotism, IT IS THEIR RIGHT, IT IS THEIR DUTY, TO THROW OFF SUCH GOVERNMENT, and to provide new Guards for their future security.-